DISCOVER YOUR TREASURE

20 KEYS TO SUCCESS

ROBERT A FIACCO

JAICO PUBLISHING HOUSE

Ahmedabad Bangalore Bhopal Bhubaneswar Chennai
Delhi Hyderabad Kolkata Lucknow Mumbai

Published by Jaico Publishing House
A-2 Jash Chambers, 7-A Sir Phirozshah Mehta Road
Fort, Mumbai - 400 001
jaicopub@jaicobooks.com
www.jaicobooks.com

Published in arrangement with
WriteLife Publishing
960 Oaktree Blvd, Christianburg
Virginia 24073, United States

To be sold only in India, Bangladesh, Bhutan,
Pakistan, Nepal, Sri Lanka and the Maldives.

DISCOVER YOUR TREASURE
ISBN 978-81-8495-863-8

First Jaico Impression: 2017

Printed by
Gopsons Papers Limited
A-2 & 3, Sector 64
Noida - 201 301 (U.P.)

In memory of
Julianna Heil Kozsan,
loving mother of eight
and the best mother-in-law
a man could hope for.

Introduction

Why am I writing this book? Over the past thirty-eight years as I have made my way through the world, I have stumbled and I have fallen; I have also won and tasted the fruits of success and victory. Along the way, I have questioned myself and the path I was on. At times, I felt as if the world had a "buried treasure" of secrets that were being kept from me. I searched for a map and key to unlock this hoard of knowledge that would yield me wealth, happiness, and peace of mind. This search has taken me to many places and exposed resources that, if I had less desire to win in life, I might have never discovered.

I'm also writing this book because it is my great hope to share the knowledge I have uncovered and to provide you with the "keys" to unlock the treasures your heart desires. I will share some of my personal experiences, as I feel I am an average person who has had common challenges all individuals can relate to. Throughout each chapter, you will also find treasure chests. They highlight the points I consider most pertinent, and can act as markers on your journey through the book.

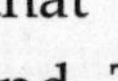

As you read, you will notice some of my writing relates to sales. This is because my career path has led me into this field and it has become my great passion. Teaching, training, and inspiring sales representatives have become my life's work; however, I truly believe my words will help you no matter your profession or the dreams you may have. You see, the principles of success are universal and consistent, regardless of your path.

The keys that I will share in this book I have discovered through my life's journey, which I am happy to say still goes on. I have discovered many of the keys from reading and studying the habits of successful men and women (both living and deceased), being mentored by successful individuals at different times in my life, and certainly by trial and error.

My journey has been both fascinating and frustrating. The search for the treasure has been an adventure I would not change for all the riches in the world. It is the journey and the search, not the treasure, that provides the great spice in life.

I hope you find this book helpful in your journey. I hope it will give you pause, make you laugh, and most importantly, help you find the treasure that you're searching for.

Table of Contents

The key and its purpose as you read

As I have traveled on my journey to uncover the treasures that life wanted to share with me, I have learned many lessons. Some I have learned the hard way through tough experiences, and others through teachers that I have met along the road. There are many important things that I would like you to take away from this book. Each chapter represents one of the twenty keys I believe can help you achieve your goals. I hope this will assist you in your search.

— Bob

Chapter One
Acknowledging Fear

Fear, more than any other single issue, holds people back in life. Fear comes in many forms and has many faces:

1. **Fear of failure**
2. **Fear of success**
3. **Fear of rejection**
4. **Fear of loss**
5. **Fear of change**

No matter what the fear is that we harbor in our minds, or how foolish it may be, it is real and it can paralyze us in our lives.

In the 1981 film *The Four Seasons,* starring Alan Alda and Carol Burnett, there is a wonderful scene where a neurotic Jack Weston is in deep conversation with his friend Alda regarding his innermost fears. It goes something like this:

> I'm ten years older than you, right? I just hope that when you get to be my age, you don't smell the foul breath of death and disintegration hanging over your shoulder the way I find it hanging over

> mine. I mean, I go to sleep at night on an ache so bad that it simply will not go away. I wake up in the middle of the night sweating, hearing my own bones decay. I have shifted into a state of entropy that's progressing geometrically. Do you have any idea—any idea—what it is to be afraid of death? I can't eat my bowl of cereal in the morning because I have an irrational fear of milk. I stand there in hallways afraid to press strange elevator buttons. I almost threw away my jockey shorts because I have this fear of elastic![1]

Although funny, this scenario is played out, to one extent or another, in all of our lives.

I certainly hope no one reading this is afraid of his or her underwear; although I'm sure my wife at times has been terrified of mine. But, this shows us the depth of fear, which can creep into the hearts and souls of many individuals. And regardless of how ridiculous it may seem to you and me, to the person facing these fears, they are real and they can be paralyzing.

Fear, as I said, is the greatest single thing that holds us back in life. Fear can be overcome, but it is not always easy.

When I first started in sales, the fear I had was overwhelming. I probably had all five of the "faces of fear"

---

1 *The Four Seasons*, Directed by Alan Alda. Universal Pictures, 1981.

just mentioned, and I wore them unknowingly at some point along the way. Here was a typical day in the early part of my career:

Well here I am, my first day as a new sales agent and I've got to make that first phone call. Man, do I hate telemarketers. I don't want to be hated . . . I wonder if I call this person if he will hate me . . . gee I hope not. No, that can't be—all these other guys in the office call people and I like them, mostly. Except that one guy—he's such a know-it-all, I wish he would shut up in the meetings. I'm gonna get a cup of coffee. Okay, let me get started. If I call, what's the worst thing that could happen? Well, I guess the person could come and find me and kill me! No, that probably wouldn't happen . . . would it? No way. Okay, the worst thing is they might hang up on me . . . that's awfully rude to hang up on someone. Well, that's probably what I would do if a telemarketer called me . . . man, I hate telemarketers. I wonder if there are any donuts left in the break room.

When I first started in the sales profession, I showed up at the office two days in a row and they made me the manager. Back then, that's sort of how it was done; I'm not sure it's much different today. Since that time, I have seen hundreds, if not thousands, of individuals come and go in my industry. To figure out what makes one person successful while so many seem to fail is an issue for all industries, not only sales. Clearly, the answer is not an easy one. It certainly could be written off as a lack of motivation, especially by a manager looking for a quick answer to a more serious problem. Now I'm not going to say there are not some of us who—some days—may need a little extra inspiration from time to time; but I do find it hard to believe a person would choose to take any career position if they did not have some desire to succeed.

I think the problem is much deeper than just lack of motivation—and my feelings are based on my personal experience. In every position I have ever held—from construction (my first job) to sales—in each opportunity, I was overcome with fear. Now, you may be asking, "Why would you be afraid, and what were you afraid of?" We will explore this issue later. First, it is imperative to acknowledge fear does, in fact, exist in our minds, and at some level it will affect our ability to perform.

Let's first try and understand the fears that affect our lives. And once this has been accomplished, we can look at how to acknowledge these fears.

We all fear something: spiders, heights, public speaking (to name just a few). While these fears can be inconvenient and certainly burdensome, they do not normally hold us back in life or business. I call these "faces of fear" because in most cases, we recognize them and are willing to discuss them. And most of the time, we can work around them.

The fears that are the most destructive in our lives I refer to as "faceless fears." I refer to them this way because they may not be obvious to us. Many times, we will not be honest and admit to ourselves that they exist. And sometimes these fears are buried so deep in our subconscious that their destruction in our lives is tantamount to guerrilla warfare against our success.

Faceless fears hold us back from moving forward in our careers and our lives in general. They can cause us to unconsciously undermine our efforts to be successful and happy. It is quite possible to live our whole lives under the oppression of these faceless tyrants. So let's discuss five of the most serious faceless fears:

1. Fear of failure

It is common to not want to fail in our endeavors, but we must not allow the fear of failing to stop us from trying. Failure is subjective in each person's mind. What one person sees as failure another person may see as a learning experience. Why is succeeding so important? Certainly, we want to be successful for the sake of being successful: making money, having a better lifestyle, and self-satisfaction. I realize in my own life that much of my struggle to win was not rooted so much in my personal quest, but more to prove something to someone else. Fear would stop me from trying because many naysayers would tell me, "This can't be done," or, "You will never do that, it's foolish." My fear was predicated not on my own desire to win, but on the fear of what others might think when I failed. The tragedy, I learned over the years, was that my fears were unfounded. When it is all said and done, nobody really cares but you. So, to be held prisoner by the fear of what others think is a true loss of happiness in one's life.

2. Fear of success

If there is one fear that is the most challenging and hardest to face up to, it is the fear of success. Few of us will admit to it and even fewer are willing to discuss this issue. We could probably substitute "deserving" for "fear." I believe that many individuals just don't believe they deserve to be successful.

These poor self-image issues are difficult to uncover and even more difficult to face up to. They may stem from real or unreal perceptions that have been with us since childhood. I can personally testify to the power and destruction this fear can cause in one's life. When I was growing up, I was hospitalized with physical issues that stopped me from participating in some sports during my childhood. Although my parents never allowed me to feel sorry for myself, I was always expected to do my best. My sibling would be punished for not succeeding, but I was always just asked, "Did you try your best?" Now, this may sound foolish, but I grew up believing I was supposed to try hard but not win. This fear can be overcome. It takes time, honesty with one's self, and sometimes professional help.

3. Fear of rejection

Let's be honest, no one likes to be rejected. It starts

when we are young; you go to the junior high dance and stand in the corner. Why? We are sure we will be told no, so we don't ask the pretty girl to dance. A similar thing can happen to ladies with young men they like. Even just saying "hi" can be a challenge sometimes. The fear of rejection is particularly devastating if you are in sales but can truly affect any career or life. The fear of not wanting to express yourself for fear of being ridiculed can hamper growth in any job you have. The difference between fear of failure and fear of rejection is self-image. Rejection is truly a deep and personal emotion that can be frightening.

The key to dealing with this fear is to try to understand why someone may be rejecting you or your idea. Most times, it has nothing to do with you personally: They may not understand, not be interested, or have their own issues they are dealing with at the moment. Once we understand that idea, we can deal with the "no" on a less personal basis and can move forward.

4. Fear of loss

One thing I have learned in my life is that as my career moved forward I had to leave certain things behind. To gain in life, most times you have to give something up. Now most of the time these things are not good for you. But most humans don't like giving anything up, good or bad. It is important we realize that to grow, what we will gain, in most cases, is much better than what we give up. It helps to look at it as a trade instead of a loss—a trade that will enrich your life. Let me share an example. I recently underwent gastric bypass surgery and lost eighty-seven pounds. During the preparation for the surgery I had to see a physiologist, and during our conversations she asked how I felt about my size. I realized that although I did not like being overweight, I received a certain level of comfort from being big and intimidating. To lose weight I had to leave that behind.

5. Fear of change

One of the most difficult actions for any individual to do is change. Change comes with uncertainty and difficulty. And sometimes changes are emotional, physical, or both. What compounds the fear of change for some people is their own uncertainty about making a change at all in their lives, no matter what form that change may take.

The major step in overcoming the fear of change is making the decision that we want to change and deciding that change will affect our lives positively. Overcoming fear of any type is not easy. It takes courage, willpower, and persistence. The first step is recognizing that we have fear and want to unburden ourselves. We can all enrich our lives by taking the first step in conquering our fears by this acknowledgment of the possibility that fear does exist in our lives. I find it fascinating that so many refuse to admit that the possibility does exist, much less that they actually do have internal fears. Maybe they feel that admitting it would make them look vulnerable or weak. Regardless of the reason, denial will simply hold you back—this I know firsthand. In my early years, I would read books, listen to tapes (CDs) and attend seminars, always looking somewhere else other than internally. When I finally had the courage to look inside and be honest with myself, I was then able to address the fears that held me back for so many years.

CHAPTER TWO

Overcoming Fear

It's midnight. The night is cold and damp. A wet drizzle is coming down as your windshield wipers slide back and forth, clearing your view as you make your way down an unfamiliar road in an unknown area of town—an area you would prefer not to be driving through in the darkness of this night. You hear a thump. Your vehicle makes a slight swerve and starts to hobble down the road—a flat tire? You pull over angrily and get out to assess the damage. As you stand staring down at the flat tire, something gets your attention. You notice three figures appear out of the shadows. Talking in a low hush, they stand and watch you, then momentarily start to walk toward you. Your heart starts to pound, your breathing quickens, and as your instincts kick in, you're thinking the worst. Do you run or dig in? As they get closer, the fear builds up inside. Not quite knowing what to do, you're prepared to act.

Approaching you, one of the three asks, "Do you need any help?"

"No thanks, I have it," you respond, as they walk past and move on down the empty, darkened street.

What just took place was fear in its purest form. Unfounded but instinctive to all mankind, it is known as the "the fight or flight response," and is an internal survival reaction common to all animals. Caused by a chain reaction in the brain that starts with an unfamiliar, unknown, stressful situation, this response to fear completes with the release of chemicals that force a racing of the heart; increased, uncontrolled breathing; and a tightening of the muscles.[2]

Now, let's have the same scenario in your own neighborhood; this time, three of your friends walk down the street to help you. What is the difference? Well, first, you know your neighbors and the neighborhood. But the real issue is your brain knows what to expect, and your brain does not draw any conclusions about something fearful happening if it senses no danger.

In the first situation, there really was no danger; but because of the unknown, your mind started to manufacture situations that were dangerous, based on past realities.

Although fear is part of human nature, many fears are learned from birth and are nurtured as we grow. Remember that anything learned can, in fact, be unlearned.

Why do I start out this book discussing fear? Perhaps you are in that ten to fifteen percent group of people who have already figured out their fears and no longer struggle with this issue. If you are, congratulations and keep up

---

2 Karl Albrecht, "Fear," *Psychology Today*, March (2012).

the great work. This discussion is primarily aimed at those eighty-five to ninety percent of us who are still working through fears and challenges. I have certainly had my share of fears to overcome in life.

Let's talk about how to overcome fear and free ourselves to win:

1. Take small steps

Sometimes when fear seems overwhelming, taking small steps "toward the fear" can help greatly. An example is cold calling on the telephone. Calling to set an appointment can be paralyzing. A suggestion is, prior to trying to set an appointment, call and do a survey with your prospect before asking for an appointment. It doesn't have to be a long survey: maybe only five questions that will help you gather information. So when you do call back to ask for the appointment, you will have information to discuss. Perhaps your great fear is giving presentations at work; it makes you physically ill. Try making small comments in meetings and working your way up to full presentations. This doesn't just apply to business situations. Whatever task you're afraid of can be broken down into smaller steps.

2. Get positive inspiration daily

Looking for small inspirational messages that you can review daily along with your goals (we'll discuss goals in Chapter Six) can help you to stay focused on the *prize* and not the *price*. Listening to motivational CDs or webinars, reading a short passage from an inspirational book, or reviewing your life goals daily can inspire you to action. Lastly, take a few minutes in the morning to write down what you will gain by attacking your fears and overcoming them. If we can reframe our view of failure and look at setbacks differently, we can unshackle our lives and open up vast opportunities for ourselves.

3. Look at failure or rejection in a different light

There is a lot of truth to the saying that every "no" brings you that much closer to a "yes." I have always believed that everything happens for a reason and a purpose that serves us. If we failed in a business or a relationship, we could say "I'm a failure," or we could say, "This just wasn't the right business or person for me." The power of how we choose to look at things has such a great bearing on our lives and our futures. Once, when my son was playing Little League Baseball, there were two outs. His team was down by one run and the bases were loaded. To the devastation of his overzealous father, he struck out. I went over to console him and said something to the effect of "don't feel bad because you struck out and you were the last batter, Son." He said, "I wasn't the last batter. There were guys behind me; they just didn't get a chance to bat." It's all in your perspective.

4. Live for the moment

Try not to allow yourself to get trapped in what has been or might be. Even though we may have had setbacks in the past, we must not allow our minds to feel the problems of the past will be the reality of the future. If you have strong goals and dreams, and you live for the moment, stay positive, and anticipate success, you will achieve it.

5. Be willing to accept change in your life

I talked about the fear of change in Chapter One. Now here is the great paradox: to overcome fear we must incorporate one of our fears into the steps it takes to actually move forward. Let me explain. Fear of success is real and comes from our fear of having to leave what we know, good or bad. None of us like to change. In fact, it is possibly one of the hardest things we do in our lives. Think of someone in a bad relationship or maybe a bad job. Why don't they just leave? It's not easy, that's why. The physical act of leaving is not nearly as difficult as the emotional challenges of leaving. Once you are willing to change, you must be patient. Change does not happen overnight. Take small steps and be patient.

6. Focus on what you want out of life

Ask yourself why you are doing this. If you know what you want out of life and understand what you must do to get there, then all that needs to be done is to stay focused on the task at hand.

7. Find out what good can be done for others, and do it

We need to understand that when we are successful, the impact that we can have on others can be immeasurable. With success comes the opportunity to help others, mentor those trying to succeed, and impact younger individuals as they try to discover their treasure. By taking our eyes off ourselves and focusing on helping others, our fears fade and disappear.

8. Take action

Action can help overcome fear. When your dreams are bigger than your fears, you can do anything. Set goals, review them, and keep them in front of you. Take action and never give up.

There is a deep correlation between worry and fear. I would like to take the time in this chapter to discuss this correlation. Worry can very easily turn into fear and eventually be that "one thing" that destroys your success in life. Remember from earlier that fear is caused by an internal reaction to perceived or real danger.

So what is worry? Webster's Dictionary defines worry as "thoughts, images, and emotions of a negative nature in which mental attempts are made to avoid anticipated potential threats." The problem is that much worry is spent on threats that never happen.

Now, I must admit that I have always been a worrier. In fact, my family has always said I worry about not having anything to worry about! My thinking has always been better to worry and have nothing happen, than not worry and be surprised. Silly, isn't it?

Worry is a useless emotion and serves no purpose but to cause anxiety that can affect you emotionally, as well as physically.

Dr. Edward Hallowell, psychiatrist and author of *Worry*, points out two specific types of worry: "toxic worry" is the kind that can cause you to paralyze yourself; "wise worry" is the type that leads to constructive action.[3]

Here are five steps to deal with worry:

1. Have "worry time"

Set a certain amount of time aside each day to worry. By this, I don't mean let negative thoughts into your head randomly. If they come, write them down and say "I'll think about this later." Don't waste a lot of time and keep yourself in a constant state of negativity.

2. Determine if you can fix it

Ask yourself if what you're worrying about can be fixed. If it can, then put a plan in action. If not, then ask yourself, "What does worrying about something that is out of my control do for me?" I tend to worry about not doing everything in my power to solve a problem. When you have a plan, you don't need to worry.

3 Edward Hallowell, *Worry*. (New York: Ballantine Books, 1998).

3. Realize stuff will happen

We need to come to the realization that stuff will happen and we can deal with it if and when it comes. If we worry about nothing (as I tend to do), we put ourselves into a state of mind that is not productive. We need to always be prepared for the unexpected, but not dwell on things that have not and may never happen. If something does come up, then formulate a plan at that time and deal with it.

4. Challenge negative thoughts

When negativity enters our thought process, we need to challenge it. Is it real or are we making it up? It is not possible to have negative thoughts in your mind at the same time you have positive thoughts there. Work to keep the negative thoughts out and focus on the positive that is and that can be.

5. Don't allow people to put snakes in your head

It absolutely amazes me how well-intentioned individuals can put thoughts in our heads that can grow like weeds and cause us needless worry and anxiety. When you see these people, run like hell.

We must face our fears to reach our true potential in life; but we must never forget to pull the small seedlings of worry up by the roots, before they grow to full size in our lives.

To borrow the title from a Bobby McFerrin song from the eighties, "Don't Worry Be Happy!"

CHAPTER THREE

Finding Inspiration

When I wake up in the morning, the only thing that I need is to be inspired; everything else will take care of itself. I struggle to understand why some individuals say "I don't need any rah-rah stuff." Hey, life is not about the X's and O's that corporate America believes. The engine that drives all innovation, production, and success in the world is passion and inspiration. I have noticed in my career that what people won't do for money, they will do for a cause or a team that they are passionate about. Finding inspiration is the first step to long-term success; and sustaining that inspiration throughout our lives is of paramount importance to success.

The issue is how to find inspiration day in and day out, especially in business and life, where we face ups and downs on a continuous basis. Certainly, we can seek out motivational speakers and read positive mental attitude (in sales lingo, PMA) books; these are truly great tools to take advantage of. I have also found that I can receive great inspiration from stories that have nothing to do with sales or business, about ordinary individuals (men and women) who overcame great obstacles to achieve lofty dreams.

I recently watched the movie *Cinderella Man*, the true story of James J. Braddock, who in the 1930s was an impoverished ex-prizefighter. At a time when millions of Americans were suffering through the bitter hardships of the Great Depression, Jim Braddock was physically and financially broken. Unable to fight or find work, he was forced to go on government relief and was barely able to provide the basic necessities for his family. He was at one point forced to send his children to live with relatives because he could not afford to feed them or keep the electricity on during the bitter, cold winters of New Jersey.

Through a twist of fate, and what would turn out to be the luckiest break of his life, James Braddock was given a chance to fight one last fight. This one was against an up-and-coming heavyweight contender whose opponent had injured himself and was unable to fight. So Braddock got the opportunity. The fight was expected to be a no contest, with the aging and injured Braddock not lasting a round. Braddock had other ideas, knocking out John "Corn" Griffin in the third round!

Inspired by the opportunity to provide for his family and going against all odds, he would win fights against the next three heavyweight contenders, eventually leading to a title fight with undefeated Max Baer, who had killed one opponent in the ring. A ten-to-one underdog in the fight, arthritic, and with injured ribs, James J. Braddock would prevail in the greatest upset in boxing history, defeating Baer in a fifteen-round unanimous decision. Braddock would pay back, with interest, all of the money he had received from the federal relief program, adding to his mystique.

There are so many inspirational scenes in the movie that can force a tear from my eyes, but the most meaningful was a scene where Braddock and his wife, Mae, were being interviewed prior to the Max Baer fight. A sports writer asked the question, "Jimmy, you couldn't win a fight for anything five years ago. How do you explain this incredible comeback?"

Braddock answered, "Now I know what I'm fighting for."

The sportswriter asked, "What you're fighting for? What are you fighting for?"

Braddock answered, "The milk money."[4]

You see, Braddock's sole motivation was the thought of needing to feed his family. A quote attributed to Bradford Merrill fits Braddock's situation: "Hardship, poverty, and want are the best incentives, and the best foundation, for the success of man."

So many individuals search for happiness and success in life but refuse to accept what the one simple key to that success is. Know what you are fighting for, and you can find inspiration. History has proven over and over that

---

4 *Cinderella Man*. Directed by Ron Howard. Universal Pictures, 2005.

eighty-five to ninety percent of the world will just get by. It's in the numbers everywhere you care to look: ten percent of salespeople make eighty percent of all sales;[5] ten percent or less of the population makes over $100,000 per year;[6] and less than two percent of individuals playing college football or basketball with aspirations of turning professional will actually make it.[7] Individuals that seemingly have the same ability, and sometimes less, somehow rise to enter that elite ten percent.

Well, despite all the statistics and data, people fail to understand what the key to success in the world really is. Individuals, and even companies, search and search for the "magic bullet" when it's so simple to see. If it has to be boiled down to one thing and one thing alone, it's inspiration that will drive the motivation to fuel all the other things required to be in that seemingly elusive ten percent elite group. Inspiration can change good companies into great companies; inspiration can change lives and even the world.

I'm so tired of seeing people whine and complain about not getting what they want out of life while they stumble through it, refusing to understand that it is their own lack of inspiration that holds them back.

---

5 Nusair Bawla, "Don't Give Up: Why Sales Persistence Pays Off." *Business News Daily*. October (2013): Web. http://www.businessnewsdaily.com/5389-in-sales-persistence-pays-off.html.

6 Kevin Short, "Everyone in America is Even More Broke Than You Think," *The Huffington Post*, November (2013): Web. http://www.huffingtonpost.com/2013/11/05/income-inequality-crisis_n_4221012.html.

7 "Probability of Competing Beyond High School," NCAA.org., last updated September 2013 http://www.ncaa.org/about/resources/research/probability-competing-beyond-high-school.

What right do I have to be giving this kind of advice? Certainly, there are many people more successful than I am, who have had greater struggles. But I would gladly trade my pack of problems for most anyone else's. In my life, I have overcome physical challenges that have led to emotional struggles. I have faced financial problems, loss of loved ones, and dealt with health issues. Through it all, the one constant factor that has always sustained me and allowed me to move forward toward my dreams has been the ability to keep myself inspired every day.

I learned many years ago that I could never motivate anyone. Motivating someone is the act of attempting to entice the person to do something that he or she is either unwilling or unable to do. What I have tried to do in my life is inspire others.

The word *inspired* means "to be in spirit." It is an internal spark that will move you to actions and thoughts that may otherwise not surface. The words *motivation* and *inspiration* are often used interchangeably, but they are simply not the same.

Motivation often is required to drive people to take an action that they do not want to take, or to do something they feel that they need to do. It is usually not driven by an internal passion to perform.

Inspiration comes from deep within someone's heart, and so, is usually looked on by that person as something that he or she is compelled to do, driven by an urge deep within.

Here are places to find inspiration:

1. Nature

2. The Internet

3. Possibility thinking

4. Other people

5. Your inner self

6. Meditation, church, or prayer

Motivation is a process of "beating" yourself into doing something, while the possibility for inspiration is everywhere in life, if you will allow yourself to let it in. Wake up every morning and ask to be inspired. Ask to inspire someone else, and see what can happen in your life.

I truly believe that inspiration comes from within and can be found all around us in the most unusual places. This inspiration is critical to light the fire of motivation in our lives.

Remember what you are fighting for. To help keep you inspired in life, here are several things most everyone fights for:

1. Our finances

We "fight" for money and what it can do for us financially, both on a personal level and for what having money can allow us to do for others. I certainly believe that money cannot buy happiness, but if you are planning on walking around on this planet it sure comes in handy.

2. Our families

We "fight" to provide a better lifestyle, better college educations for our children, and most importantly, the quality of life we can have by being able to spend quality time with our families and not be a slave to someone else's clock. When my son was playing high school football, I never missed a practice or a game. That's quality of life.

3. Our fellow man

Most businesses and industries, no matter what the type, have an impact on something in the world. You may can cranberries in a factory. Or clean office buildings. What does that have to do with anything? More than you may realize. Who wants to go to an office with dirty floors? And cranberries are part of many Thanksgiving meals each year. Whatever product or service you provide is helping or enriching someone, somewhere. It may be a very small impact, but that impact may have a profound effect on someone you may never meet.

A career is not a job. If you only feel like you have a job then you will probably never be totally happy, fulfilled, or inspired. My advice is find something you are passionate about.

The toll of success in life is great but so are the rewards. Focus on why you are here and let it carry you through the hard times. Let inspiration flow. It is so worth it.

Chapter Four

Staying Inspired

Finding inspiration for a day or a week is one thing, but sustaining inspiration in our lives is a totally different story. It is particularly difficult because, as I stated in the previous chapter, inspiration comes from within. The outside forces that I listed can help kindle the flame inside of us, but to have an inferno deep inside your heart that lasts a lifetime is truly a gift.

Look at the late Nelson Mandela as an example of how a man could endure hardship. He did it for twenty-five-plus years and never gave in to taking the easy way, even when offered pardon for letting go of his dream of a free South Africa.[8] He had an inspiration deep in his heart and soul; and this, I feel, is a true blessing all of us should strive to find in our lives.

I heard somewhere that "Dreams are what make life tolerable."[9] I think that a truer statement has never been made. Setting goals in our lives gives us focused purpose and a mission. Dreams and goals can, and will, carry

---

8 "Biography of Nelson Mandela," The Nelson Mandela Foundation. https://www.nelsonmandela.org/content/page/biography.

9 *Rudy*. Directed by David Anspaugh. TriStar Pictures 1993.

us through the hardest of times and cause that internal inspiration.

If we look at ultra-successful individuals in life who have achieved what they feel is the pinnacle of success, why is it that so many of these same individuals turn to drugs and alcohol? I think the answer can be found in the fact that if we are not growing, then we are dying. No matter where we are in life, we can always be more. We can be more giving, more caring, and more loving. The key is never giving up on your goals and dreams, and always stretching to grow, be it financially, career-wise, spiritually, or emotionally.

Here are four simple ways to get your blood pumpin' and your butt jumpin' every day:

1. Music

They say music soothes the savage beast. Well, it also can get you energized and pumped up to attack the world. Why do you think so many high-performing athletes have iPods plugged into their ears before competing? Think of the excitement and enthusiasm of a rock concert. Find your favorite music to listen to when you need a pick-me-up and let it "rock your world."

2. Words

They are powerful and can stir the soul. Find a source of short, motivational quotes that energize you.

3. Laughter

It is impossible to laugh and be down at the same time. We all need to get daily doses of laughter as much as possible. We can find humor on the Internet, television, or the daily comic strips. It's everywhere. We just need to look and laugh.

4. Stories

There are so many inspirational true stories out there in the world. Every day there are individuals performing heroic deeds, overcoming hardships, and winning in life against overwhelming odds. These stories, if we allow them, will make us feel like we can conquer the world.

In the song "Flashdance . . . What a Feeling" by Irene Cara, there is a line about passion. The simplicity of that line is overwhelmingly inspiring, but the implementation of this thought can cause heartache, anxiety, and frustration. The mere fact that you have a dream can cause you heartache if you don't have the courage to take steps to fulfill that dream, and make that passion a reality. Who wants to live with regret over what could have been? Sometimes, this is why so many unhappy souls seem to float through life with seemingly no idea of what their passion is. Some people are afraid to articulate what their passion is, because of the fear they may have. They could fail or be ridiculed. To these folks, it's better to leave their passions buried. The comment "I just don't know what I want to do with my life!" is repeated so often by so many that it seems inborn in mankind. Or could it be that people do know but are afraid to act?

Over my years, in my life and career, I have met people of all ages that are frustrated over the life they live, feeling they are trapped with no opportunity to fulfill their purpose, much less even work toward it. These individuals feel they are trapped in an endless future of work that will leave them unfulfilled and unhappy.

What causes this to happen to so many, so often? Let me give you this to ponder: Many times we believe inspiration should come first and the work and toil will follow because of the inspiration we have for the project we have undertaken. What if, in fact, it was the work, toil, and sweat that caused the long-lasting inspiration to continue? And passion for whatever pursuit we undertook actually grew from the work we did toward that result?

If the secret to long-term inspiration in your life was action toward your dreams and goals, what should you do? If you are waiting for inspiration to take hold so you can move forward, you could be waiting for a bus that is not making your stop. Take action and see what can happen in your life.

Here are five inspirational examples of individuals who had dreams that would eventually shape the future of the world:

1. Nelson Mandela

Born in South Africa in 1918, he fought a lifelong battle to end apartheid (a system of complete racial separation) in South Africa. This amazing man spent eighteen years in the most horrible prison conditions imaginable, twice refusing release in exchange for renouncing the attack on apartheid. After his release from prison, Mandela would go on to become the first black president of South Africa, winning South Africa's first all-race election. He would share the Nobel Peace Prize in 1993 with the South African President F.W. de Klerk.[10]

2. Ronald Reagan

"Tear down this wall!" On June 12, 1987, President Ronald Reagan, against the advice of many of his advisors—and at a time of heightened tensions between East and West—gave a historic speech at the Brandenburg Gate near the Berlin Wall. The speech challenged Soviet Union leader Mikhail Gorbachev to destroy the wall. The thought, although absurd, was part of the Reagan ideology that there could be a Communist-free government in the East. Twenty-nine months later, on November 9, 1989, East Germany would, in fact, open the Berlin Wall. This action would be the start of the dismantlement of the Communist

---

10 "Biography of Nelson Mandela," The Nelson Mandela Foundation. https://www.nelsonmandela.org/content/page/biography.

governments of Eastern Europe and eventually the entire Soviet Union.[11]

3. Mahatma Gandhi

Albert Einstein said of Gandhi "Generations to come will scarce believe that such a one as this ever in flesh and blood walked upon this earth."[12] A quiet, unassuming man, Gandhi led a revolution against colonialism of India, professing and living a life of peace and nonviolence. His commitment to change through peace was truly inspirational to the likes of Martin Luther King, Jr.[13]

4. Rosa Parks

Born in 1913 in Tuskegee, Alabama, this one woman's courage to stand up to the establishment by refusing to give up her seat on a Montgomery, Alabama bus to a white passenger would spur a citywide boycott. The city would eventually be forced to lift the law requiring segregation on public buses. This single action by one individual would help launch the civil rights movement.[14]

---

11 Peter Robinson, "Tear Down This Wall: How Top Advisers Opposed Reagan's Challenge to Gorbachev—But Lost." *National Archives*. (Summer 2007, Vol. 39, No. 2). Web. http://www.archives.gov/publications/prologue/2007/summer/berlin.html.

12 "Quotable quotes under 'Albert Einstein'," Goodreads.com, http://www.goodreads.com/quotes/131951-generations-to-come-will-scarce-believe-that-such-a-one.

13 Gadadhara Pandit Dasa, "Martin Luther King Jr. and Gandhi: The Liberating Power of Non-violence." *The Blog* (blog), ***The Huffington Post***. January 21, 2014 http://www.huffingtonpost.com/gadadhara-pandit-dasa/martin-luther-king-jr-and_3_b_4631610.html.

14 "Rosa Parks," History.com. Web. http://www.history.com/topics/black-history/rosa-parks

5. Mother Teresa

Also known as the Blessed Teresa of Calcutta, she founded the Missionaries of Charity, a Roman Catholic organization, which in 1997 had almost 4,000 members in over 120 countries, including a chapter in New York founded exclusively for AIDS patients.[15] The peace and comfort that she has brought to the world is nothing short of phenomenal and inspirational for everyone.

These short writings about these great people certainly cannot do justice to their inspiring lives and the amazing impact that they have had on the world. They are great examples of what one person taking action with a dream can do to impact history and inspire generations, when they themselves are inspired.

15 "Mother Teresa of Calcutta," *Catholic Online* http://www.catholic.org/clife/teresa.

CHAPTER FIVE

Developing a Winning Attitude

The attitude of the individuals in an organization determines the culture within that organization.[16] And that culture will ultimately decide the success or failure of the organization. So many senior leaders believe that the numbers needed to affect the bottom line lie (as I stated in Chapter Three) strictly in the X's and O's (the "how to") of the business. But the culture of an organization has as much to do with the success as the how to. Whether in a sports team or corporation, the attitude of the members of an organization will determine how the organization will rise, and whether everyone involved will win.

What do an apple and a professional have in common? One bad one can spoil the whole bunch. Attitude is contagious. A positive one can ignite an army and change the world; a bad one can be like a disease. One individual with a bad attitude can, without remorse, infiltrate an organization and steal the dreams of many good people. In business, it is so important to protect and defend your

---

16 Michael Watkins, "What is Organizational Culture? And Why Should We Care?" *Harvard Business Review*. May 15, 2013. https://hbr.org/2013/05/what-is-organizational-culture/.

attitude with all you have. You should run—yes, run—from anyone the first time you hear negativity come from him or her. A seed of negativity passed on to someone can grow and take root like a weed in a garden, and before you are aware of it, you are overrun with negativity. I am not saying there will not be legitimate issues that need to be addressed and dealt with, but to have someone that continually complains and never looks for a solution to the problem can do nothing good for anyone. I don't know what it is about human nature that perpetuates the need to give someone advice that is directly in conflict with his or her dreams. I have seen it hundreds of times if I have seen it once . . . someone dares to believe they can be more, and there is always someone who feels the need to tell them why they can't.

Let me share several tips to help you protect your attitude:

1. Run from anyone who wants to spew negativity into your mind.

2. Check the "fruit on the tree."

If you're going to take advice, check to see how successful the person giving it is.

3. Read or listen to something positive every day.

4. Don't look to others to validate your dreams. Listen to your heart.

Faith and belief are fundamental to one's attitude and

cannot be avoided in any facet of our lives. If you have no faith or belief in what you do, it is hard to have a good attitude, much less sustain yourself through the hard times. So often, faith and belief are intertwined, and many times, misunderstood; while they are in fact very closely related, they are distinctly different in their meanings. The definitions are as follows:

Faith is confidence or trust in a person, thing, deity, or in the doctrine or teachings of a religion. It may also be a belief that is not based on truth.

Belief is the psychological state in which an individual holds a proposition to be true.

Many of my experiences have led me to feel that belief is simply a mental decision based on an opinion that something may or may not be true. It is an opinion of reality, not reality itself. Also, belief in its purest sense is a mental concept or decision.

Faith, I have come to believe, takes action. Here is a great equation on faith that I often use:

Faith = (Belief + Action + Confidence)[17]

Here is an example of the differences between faith and belief:

Belief is knowing that the planet Mars is real and

---

17 Chris, "The Difference Between Faith and Belief." Purposelydifferent.com. http://purposelydifferent.com/the-difference-between-faith-and-belief.

knowing that air flight is also real. So, I believe it would be possible to travel to Mars.

Faith is taking the actions with confidence to actually attempt to travel to Mars, with absolutely no guarantee that it is possible.

In our everyday lives, belief and faith are inescapable. We believe, when we get up in the morning and start our cars to drive to work, that we will arrive safely. This is based on the fact that we have done it hundreds of times before.

Faith normally will be called upon when the unexpected happens and we are faced with the unknown; for example, if we never make it to work because of an unfortunate accident, and surgery is required, faith kicks in (believing the surgery will help you + having the surgery [action] + confidence in your doctor).

As I stated, belief is an intellectual process; faith incorporates both mental and emotional concepts that are, most times, founded on one's inner soul. In business, as in life, belief and faith are of paramount importance. I think the challenge lies in the fact that it is easy for someone to believe that individuals can make money in sales, and that there is a demand for a specific product or service. The challenge, then, lies in someone taking action with confidence and doing the things required to sell that product or service. Sales is only one example. There are many opportunities available in the world. You just need belief and action.

I hope everyone can find faith in their lives, reaching into the depths of their souls to take action on those things they truly believe. Faith and belief can help instill a positive attitude, raising you to new heights of success and happiness.

Attitude is a fickle emotion. One moment your attitude can be high as a kite, and the next it can drop like a stone. Why is it so easy to dismantle a positive attitude? There are many issues involved. Challenges may pop up out of the blue, or other people may drag us down. Why? Who knows. Maybe it's because misery truly does love company. There are outside factors that can affect our attitude.

The more negative issues arise in our own minds—the one place we can never truly escape from. We are in our heads twenty-four hours a day, seven days a week. Even when we are asleep, our subconscious is at work. In an article in "Mind Power," John Kehoe makes a statement that, "All physical reality is made up of vibrations of energy . . . This is not a concept or theory, but rather the startling new reality that quantum physics now reveals to us. Your thoughts have a powerful influence; they affect what happens to you."[18]

If this is true, then our attitude can be controlled by the center known as our mind. The concept of our mind controlling our lives is as old as time. Yet most men and

---

18 John Kehoe, "Mind Power Basics," Learnmindpower.com, http://www.learnmindpower.com/using_mindpower/basics/.

women refuse to believe this concept, much less implement it in their lives.

Here are some steps to help you control your thoughts:

1. Know what you truly believe

Our subconscious holds the secret to our true beliefs. Work on self-awareness when negative thoughts start to overtake your mind. Keep a journal about what your instincts say you are thinking. You cannot have a great attitude if you do not believe in what you are doing.

2. Develop positive thinking habits

When negativity starts to creep into your mind, have things you can immediately think about. I have a great passion for golf, and when negative thoughts attack me, I will immediately put myself on the golf course mentally.

3. Take stock of what you have

When you list all the good that you have in your life and career, you can get reenergized about where you are in life, which helps your attitude.

Understand your mind and you can control your attitude. Run from those who would drag your attitude down and watch your life blossom.

Having a positive attitude takes work. That fact can be hard to take for some folks. There are, as I have said, many internal and external factors that affect our attitude every day. We cannot always control every factor, but we can control how we react and how we respond to these factors. Wanting to have a great attitude is a start.

Chapter Six

Establishing Written Goals

The Bible says, "For whatsoever a man soweth, that shall he also reap" (Galatians 6:7).

Whatever you plant, the crop will be abundant. The soil makes no distinction between corn and poison. Both good and bad plants can grow under the right circumstances.

The keys to success in any endeavor are vision, belief, commitment, and hard work. The focus and direction of these traits, if delivered through proper goal setting, can be unstoppable. The key is setting aggressive, reasonable goals that you can make a total commitment to. Here are the simple but complex steps to achieve this:

1. Evaluate and determine what you want to accomplish in all the important areas of your life: professional, personal, financial, and spiritual.

2. Develop a plan, step by step, to accomplish your goals. This plan should be detailed and written.

3. Once your plan has been established, make a one hundred percent commitment to the activities that are in your plan. Realize if you are not committed to doing the

activities every day, your plan will be in vain, and you will fail to reach your goal.

4. Set short-term milestones to track and monitor your progress as often as possible. You should have daily, weekly, monthly, quarterly, and annual goals to review frequently. To keep yourself on track, you must place your goals in front of you constantly.

5. Be flexible, not to the goals you have set, but to your plan to accomplish those goals. Never give up on the goals you have committed to, as long as you have given thought to them prior to setting them. But be prepared to adjust your plan of attack to accomplish them. I have seen many individuals fail because they were unwilling to change their process. We must remember the result is ultimately what matters, not how it is accomplished, as long as the method is legal and moral.

6. Accept ultimate responsibility for your success or your failure. To be honest with you, I have had years, I am sorry to say, that were not successful for me professionally. I failed to make quarterly goals and had years when I came up short of my sales objectives. It is not easy to say this or take responsibility, but I must; I must so that I can grow and assure that I have control over making my future a success. It would be easy to lay out a number of reasons for the results of any given year, and blame this or that for the poor results; and I could probably justify how I am not responsible. But I am responsible. I could have adjusted my plan of attack to win earlier in the year. The fact that I

did not is my fault alone. Now, I can take what I learned from my life challenges and assure future success.

The steps to being successful are simple; implementation of these steps can be complex and difficult without commitment, belief, and a vision of where you want to go.

There are five important reasons (I call them "The Big Five") to have written, clear goals. These five steps will help you, and in many ways, truly give you a map to success:

1. Having written, clear goals will allow you to identify what you truly want out of life. There are many things that would be nice to have; but when push comes to shove and the road gets rocky, there is a big difference between "being nice to have" and something that is a burning desire in your heart. This first step takes some true soul-searching; but if you are honest with yourself, you are well on your way to success.

2. They will inspire you to take action that will push you to reach the things you want. Keeping what you want in front of you daily will spur you to action, even when your favorite TV show is on.

3. Written goals will keep you on track when future opportunities pop up. I always say, "There are a million stories in the naked city . . . and sooner or later you will hear them all." People will try to suck you into their dreams. If your dreams are not clearly imbedded in your mind, you will jump on the first scam that comes your way.

4. They will help you overcome the hurdles that life will

put in your way. When your eyes are firmly positioned on what you want out of life, you tend to miss the potholes.

5. Well-defined goals will give you something to measure and monitor your progress in life, and allow you to enjoy the small victories along the way.

Let's talk about how to write your goals and what you should do with them after that. The key to writing goals is to be as specific and clear as possible. You don't want to say, "I want to buy a new home." You want to say something like, "I want to buy a 3,500-square-foot, all-brick home with four bedrooms and three-and-one-half baths in such-and-such neighborhood." The more specific and clearer your goals, the more you will be drawn to them, and the more your subconscious will start to develop ways to achieve them.

Once your goals are written down, it is important to keep them in front of you and review them weekly, if not daily. Constantly remind yourself of what you want. Feel what it will be like to have it. I used to write goals down, seal them in an envelope, and open them on New Year's Day. The problem was, I would forget what I had written down. One time, when we had moved and I was going through boxes, I came across about eight years of goals in envelopes. The envelopes were yellowed and worn from years of storage; as I read them, I noticed a disturbing trend. The first year, one of the goals said, "I will get my weight down to 195 pounds." The next year it read, "I will get my weight down to 200 pounds." And year three? "I will get my weight down to 220 pounds." I finally realized that if I didn't make a change, I would soon look like Jabba the Hutt. Keep your goals in front of you!

So why, if setting written goals are so important, do so few individuals actually do it? There are a number of reasons worth exploring:

1. Lack of motivation. There are just some people with no desire to improve themselves . . . it is truly sad.

2. Many individuals are in a place in life that they feel they have everything they need and are truly happy . . . good for them.

3. Fear just keeps rearing its ugly head.

4. Past setbacks. There are many individuals who have had dreams that were left unfulfilled, and now they are reluctant to dream again.

5. They just don't believe they can have what they want, or that there is true value in writing down their goals . . . how wrong they are.

6. Setting goals that other people want for them, instead of what they truly want. It is not unusual to set goals to achieve something that doesn't have true meaning to us, but to someone close to us; to try to prove something to them or impress them. The only goals that are truly worthwhile are those that come from deep in our hearts. Those are the goals that will make us jump out of bed early and work late; those are the goals that will make us lay it all on the line; and those are the only goals worth chasing.

Don't be afraid to dream and dream big. Commit

to your goals and dreams, and they really can come true. I know I said it earlier, but I will say it again: when our dreams are bigger than our fears, we can accomplish anything.

Chapter Seven
Taking Action

In the previous chapter, we discussed the importance of written goals. Taking action on those goals is the next step. But even simple actions can have a big impact. To illustrate, let's start with two well-known examples from history:

July 2, 1863. Gettysburg Pennsylvania. The 20th Maine Volunteer Infantry Regiment, commanded by Col. Joshua Lawrence Chamberlain, is charged with holding a piece of ground known by the name "Little Round Top." His orders were simple: hold Little Round Top "at all costs."[19] As the battle ensued, the 20th Maine, sustaining heavy losses, continually repelled the Confederate attacks. Holding through two final assaults by the 15th Alabama, forces depleted and ammunition all but gone, Col. Joshua Lawrence Chamberlain would take "that action at all costs," which would later earn him a Congressional Medal of Honor.

With the hill all but lost, he would order his regiment to "fix bayonets" and lead an attack down the hill that would

---

19 James R Brann, "America's Civil War: Defense of Little Round Top," *America's Civil War, November 1999.*

take the amassing Confederates by total surprise. Private Elisha Coan of the 20th would later recall "the effect was stunning, the rebel front line, at the sudden movement, thinking we had been reinforced . . . threw down their arms and cried out 'Don't fire! We surrender!' The rest fled in wild confusion."[20]

Debates would go on for years after the Battle of Gettysburg was put in the annals of history. How important was the battle at Little Round Top to the success of the war for the Union? Many historians consider it to be the key point in the battle on that day. All because one man had the courage to take action: an action that could have easily ended his life and the lives of his men.

The next example is more recent, but has an impact just as big, if not bigger:

December 1, 1955. Montgomery, Alabama. A young seamstress, returning home from a department store where she worked, took her place on a bus. Sitting in the back of the bus, as was the law, she sat in the front-most row designated for blacks. As the bus filled, the driver ordered the young lady and three others to stand and surrender their seats to white passengers boarding the bus. Three of the individuals hesitated, but gave up their seats; Rosa Parks refused. She would be arrested and fined ten dollars, plus four dollars court costs, under the city's segregated-bus ordinance. This single act of defiance to an unfair and

---

20 Stephen W. Sears, *Gettysburg*. (Massachusetts: Houghton Mifflin Harcourt, 2004), p. 295-296.

unjust law would galvanize the civil rights movement in America.[21]

Years later, Ms. Parks would say that her act was not a thought-out statement of rebellion. She had paid for her seat and the others got on the bus after her; it simply was not right.

These are just two stories of the impact an action taken by an individual can have on a country, or even the world. These acts of instinct by individuals showed courage in the face of injustice and danger. Imagine what you can do in your life by taking action.

The following story, while not about the impact on a nation, had an enormous impact on one individual and one family, and affected hundreds, if not thousands, of lives. On January 2, 1994, I had been struggling with which direction to take in my career. I had been persuaded to join another organization, but had put off the decision for several months; you see, I didn't like change in my life. And I've found that sometimes, even when you know you need to change, you just don't. As I drove to my office that cold January day, something came over me. I turned my vehicle around, drove to the regional office of the company trying to hire me, and accepted the position.

Had I not taken action, I am quite sure my life would be very different today. That position led to another with

---

21 "Rosa Parks," History.com, http://www.history.com/topics/black-history/rosa-parks.

a different company, and over the last nineteen years, I have contracted over five thousand agents into the sales industry, many of those lives have been changed forever.

Let's say that you have taken the first step and written down your goals; but for some reason you just can't find the inspiration to take action and start to improve your life. Why is that? My guess is that you really don't want it! Sometimes that can be hard to hear. I believe there are many things that would be nice to have; but "nice to have" and "have to have" are quite different motivators. As I look back over my own life, I realize that either everything I ever really wanted I have or I am still working to get. Now, there are a lot of things I thought I would like; but somewhere along the way, I decided it was either too difficult and would not be worth the cost to get or I just didn't really want it. Only you can see the desires that are deep inside of you. Once you commit to them, the subconscious goes to work to help you achieve them. But you first have to do some soul-searching and develop true, meaningful goals.

Here are several steps to help you take action in your life:

1. Make a list of everything you think you want out of life

Maybe the idea of a list with everything you want seems

far-fetched. But remember the ten percent group from Chapter Three that makes $100,000 per year? It has also been discovered that less than ten percent of Americans write down their goals.[22] Is there a correlation? There seems to be.

So, how do you write your list? Well, what do you want? If you want to be an astronaut, put it on the list. If you want to hike to the top of Mount Fuji in Japan, put that on the list. Same thing if you'd like to open a bakery. Now, set it aside for one week, then sit down and rewrite the list from memory. How many items are on both lists? If an item is on the first list, but not the second, how important is it to you? Maybe not that important. Once you have one list of the things that matter most to you, take that list, and next to each item, write down what you would be willing to do to get it. Would you move? Work twelve-hour days, seven days per week? You see, if you are not willing to sacrifice something to move ahead in life, then you are probably too comfortable where you are, and not ready to move forward.

2. Don't wait for your situation to be perfect to take action

Things will never, ever be perfect; there will always be things that come up that can pull you off track, or stop you altogether.

---

22 Ken Cheo, "Goal Setting: Why 90% of Us Don't Do It Effectively," (blog), *Boston Business Journal*, September 2012, http://www.bizjournals.com/boston/blog/mass-high-tech/2012/09/goal-setting-why-90-of-us-dont-do.html?page=all.

3. Decide to make things happen in your life

Making the decision to take action is an enormous step toward changing your life. That decision by itself has power. Thoughts and plans without action will always go unfulfilled.

4. Don't be afraid to adjust once you start moving forward

Remember "the best-laid schemes."[23] Making adjustments will help you stay on target. No plan is perfect at its inception.

5. Write down weekly action goals

They will help you take small actions toward your larger tasks. Having little lists that are a part of bigger lists and bigger goals is a tremendous help. Not everything in life can be part of your goals, but do your best to get those little things done every day.

When you take action on a well-laid out plan, there is no telling where you can go or what you can achieve.

---

23 "To A Mouse," Robertburns.org, http://www.robertburns.org/inenglish/extracts.shtml.

CHAPTER EIGHT

Building a Winning System

All great organizations have great systems in place. Listen to winning football or basketball coaches and they will talk about their offensive systems, their recruiting systems, their coaching systems. Great corporations will talk about their marketing systems or their production systems. Systems are the gasoline that drives or fuels the vehicle and keep it on track as it pursues its destination.

BusinessDictionary.com defines a system as "a set of detailed methods, procedures and routines created to carry out a specific activity, perform a duty, or solve a problem."[24]

Wouldn't it make sense, that if systems were imperative for successful organizations, the same would be true for our own lives? After all, our lives are similar to a sporting team or a corporation: We want to win, we have a profit and loss statement, and if we don't make a profit, we are most likely in financial trouble. Having winning systems, which drive our lives, can be the difference between winning or

---

24 "What is a System?" Businessdictionary.com, http://www.businessdictionary.com /definition/system.html.

losing in our endeavors. Life systems can help keep your goals on track, make your actions effective and profitable, keep you sane in your quest, and most importantly, keep balance in your life.

A successful football program has an offensive system, defensive system, special teams system; basically, every area of importance to that team will have its own unique system. Much like our lives should. I have found eight life systems covering all facets of our lives that are important to implement.

The eight winning life success systems are:

1. The vehicle

This is the first system you must establish. What is the vehicle you plan to use to get you where you want to go? Are you going to work for someone else in corporate America? If so, what is your system for advancement? And do you have a set out career path and a time frame with steps to achieve this path? Are you going to go into business for yourself? If so, is your business going to be product oriented or service oriented? If product oriented, will you sell hot dogs or hamburgers? Will you put your store on the left side of the street or the right side? Nobody teaches these little things. The system you use to manage the vehicle and figure these things out will help you stay on track and help you plan how you will drive that vehicle to success.

2. The finance system

This system is vital to survival. There are three phases to this system:

A. Budget: Do you have a written budget that you review weekly? Are you operating in the red or the black? You have to know if what you are doing is profitable (black) or not (red). Even if you have a job with a salary, if you make $45,000 per year and spend $50,000, your "business" is failing. Your budget should account for everything that comes in and goes out of your hands financially, and hopefully it's more coming in, not less.

B. Savings system: Do you have a systematic method of putting money away for emergencies? Many banking institutions have automatic systems, and small amounts can be taken out of your checking account or paycheck and put in a savings account. Regardless of the method, putting something away for a rainy day can make you free from financial worry.

C. Long-term investment system: Have you set up a long-term investment system and strategy? Many times, people believe they don't make enough to save for the future; but even the smallest amount will add up over time. Doing nothing is equivalent to surrendering to the future. Recent studies by the Social Security Administration show that the average retirement income for a baby boomer is expected to run approximately $44,000 annually.[25] This

25 "The Changing Impact of Social Security on Retirement Income in the United States," Social Security Administration website, accessed December 21, 2014, http://www.ssa.gov/policy/docs/ssb/v65n3/v65n3p1.html.

represents all income sources of a retiree: investments, savings, pensions, and social security. It does not factor in tax increases or the adjustment projected by the Social Security Administration to cut potential benefits by 2040. I cannot stress enough the need to have a financial system in your life that is reviewed frequently. If your system is failing, you may have to review your vehicle.

3. The health system

Do you have a system in place to protect your most important asset, your body? Do you have a structured exercise system? A diet regimen? If we don't schedule exercise as a regular part of our day, most times it will not get done; and all the success in the world is empty without our health.

4. The spiritual system

I hope you believe in something greater than yourself. I don't care what your religious convictions are, but having faith in something greater than "this" can sustain you through the challenges of this world. Do you have a system that allows you to be fed spiritually? It could be a church, a synagogue, or meditation. Whatever you use to find deeper meaning in life is important to your overall development.

5. The goals system

We have discussed the importance of goal setting in

Chapter Six, but I do want to reiterate the importance of having a system to set and review meaningful, attainable goals that are truly what you want out of life.

6. The growth system

In life, we are either growing or we are dying. It is important to your long-term success and ultimate happiness that you have a system to continually learn new things, in your chosen profession as well as outside the norm of your life. Learning enriches your mind and your soul. So, do you have a system to read on a regular basis? I have a goal to read so many books every month on various subjects. But reading isn't the only way to learn. You can get certifications in your field, or take college courses, either at a local college or university, or through online learning.

7. Recreation and relaxation system

How do you unwind and recharge your batteries? None of us can run full throttle and not stop for a breath now and then. Do you have a system that gives you periodic vacations and getaways for yourself or with your family? Quality of life is what it's all about.

8. The checkup system

It is crucial for you to have a system in place for your life to monitor the systems listed above. Now, you may say, "I don't need systems to do the normal functions of life." My question is, "How's it working for you?" You see, most of what is listed in the seven systems above are, in fact, normal functions of life. Why do so many people fail then? The reason, I have found, is without systems to manage our lives, things happen, and we get off track and never get focused back on the important things.

Let me restate Businessdictionary.com's definition of what a system is: "A system is a set of detailed methods, procedures and routines created to carry out a specific activity, perform a duty, or solve a problem."[26] All of the above are things that can turn into problems for people if not watched and managed. Problems can become catastrophes. By adopting winning systems early in your life, you can avoid setbacks, financial hardships, and chronic health issues; you can truly live a quality life. Remember the old saying, attributed to Benjamin Franklin: "An ounce of prevention is worth a pound of cure."

26 "What is a System?" Businessdictionary.com, http://www.businessdictionary.com /definition/system.html.

CHAPTER NINE

Visualization

Since the earliest recorded history of mankind, there has been a belief that some magical, misunderstood "force" could drive the direction of a man's or woman's life. The ancient Greeks believed in the god Hermes and spoke of the "Seven Cosmic Principles of Hermes Trismegistos" (Hermetic Laws). At its core is the concept that "The All Is Mind," explaining that all phenomena in the universe is simply a mental creation.[27]

Proverbs 23:7 states, "For as he thinketh in his heart, so is he." In Matthew 21:22 it is written "And all things, whatsoever ye shall ask in prayer, believing, ye shall receive."

In the modern era, there have been literally thousands of books written on the law of attraction and creative visualization.

History has proven that there is a deep-seated need for man to believe that he has some internal control over his fate. Even the greatest scoffers of the concept of "cosmic

27 "The Seven Cosmic Principles of Hermes Trismegistos [Hermetic Laws]," *You Create Reality* (blog), May 2007, http://youcreatereality.com/blog/index.php/category/hermetic-laws/.

direction" have dreams and goals. The moment that we think something, the possibility of it happening exists in our lives. Tony Robbins, in his world-renowned book, *Unlimited Power*, states that we create the world that we live in, good or bad.[28] This concept—that hardships, burdens, and torments in life are brought on by our own thoughts—is unsettling to most individuals. It is easier to believe that we have no control whatsoever, than to believe that we are actually mentally responsible for the bad things that take place in our lives.

To better understand this concept, I think we must start with the concept that you or I cannot just sit down and think we have a million dollars, close our eyes, and when we open them, BAM there it sits. We could only wish it were that easy! The process is more complex and takes patience. To demonstrate, let me share three stories with you:

Actor Jim Carrey, star of movies like *How the Grinch Stole Christmas, Ace Ventura,* and *Dumb and Dumber* (to name a few), was speaking at a convention in May of 2010 regarding the law of attraction and made this statement:

> I've always believed in magic. When I wasn't doing anything in this town, I'd go up every night, sit on Mulholland Drive, look out at the city, stretch out my arms, and say 'Everyone wants to work with

---

28 Anthony Robbins, *Unlimited Power: The New Science of Personal Achievement.* (New York: Simon & Schuster, 1986), p. 93.

> me. I'm a really good actor. I have all kinds of great movie offers.' I'd just repeat these things over and over, literally convincing myself that I had a couple of movies lined up. I'd drive down that hill, ready to take the world on, going, 'Movie offers are out there for me, I just don't hear them yet.'[29]

Jim Carrey believes he literally thought his way to success.

Now let's look at Oprah Winfrey. Winfrey said that after reading the book *The Color Purple* she became obsessed with it, buying copies of the book for everyone she knew. She said she was consumed by the story for months. One day she was called by her agent to read for a Steven Spielberg movie . . . *The Color Purple*. Months went by without a call, and, convinced she was refused the role because of her weight, she checked into a weight loss clinic. She said that she was so distraught that she would cry and pray. One day, while walking the track at the clinic, she got a call from none other than Spielberg himself.[30]

Oprah Winfrey believes she literally drew the part to herself.

A more personal story involves me. It's a story I have shared a lot, but I feel it bears repeating. While living in West Virginia, my wife and I had started golfing together.

---

29 "Jim Carrey: Carrey'd Away," interview by Movieline staff, *Movieline.com*, July 1, 1994, http://movieline.com/1994/07/01/carreyd-away/3/.

30 Oprah Winfrey, interview by Ann Curry, Dateline, NBC News, May 21, 2006, http://www.nbcnews.com/id/12821015/ns/dateline_nbc/t/oprah-comes-full-circle/.

After several months of playing, we decided it would make sense to join a country club. But I was not making nearly enough money to join or keep up the monthly cost. Every day for one year, I drove several miles out of my way to and from my office to the country club we wanted to join. I parked my car, sat and stared at the beautiful fairways and greens, and left. One year after starting that ritual, we were members of that country club.

I believe I willed myself to belong to that club and attracted the money required to join.

So how is it done? It seems so much easier, for some strange reason, to allow the negative possibilities to overrun our thought process, than to stay focused on the good things that we want out of life. I have found that there are several things that you can do to help keep positive visualization a part of your life:

1. Understand the age-old saying that "Good things come to those who wait." Having patience is not always easy. I believe that when we don't get what we want, when we want it, we can slip into a negative mental state, pushing away the very thing we want. You see, just because we can't get it immediately does not mean it will never happen.

2. Understand the first point. Then it will be easier for you to continue to see yourself where you want to be in life, even when you are not there yet. One fact that I have learned is that it is not possible to think something positive and negative at the same time. That's why when you can visualize to the point that you get emotionally involved

with your thoughts, negativity cannot be in your mind. This will help you to not give up on your dreams and goals.

3. Let your dreams become emotional. When I think about what I want to achieve, I can literally get myself to a point of excitement, bringing myself to tears of joy in the process.

4. Live as if you are there! Dress the part; look at the things you want: homes, cars, or whatever you dream about. Now, don't run out and spend money you don't have, but walk, talk, and act like you have it.

5. Set twenty minutes aside each day to sit quietly and "see" your life as it will be. Meditation is powerful in the process of visualization.

6. Have a "magic box." I have a box that has the words "Whatever Is In This Box Is" written on it. It's something I learned years ago, and have followed. In the box are pictures of all the things I want. I can tell you: Many things have gone into that box that have become reality in my life. When I reach a goal, one picture comes out, and another goes in. You always have to stretch and grow. New dreams help you do that.

Please do not underestimate the power of the human will and the spirit that the Creator has given each of us. The mind is a powerful tool, and the energy that flows from our thoughts is a force that has the power to create an unbelievable life for us. The opposite is that we also can use that same energy to undermine our own happiness and success. I personally believe how we choose to think about our situation is what can create happiness or despair in our lives. For some, that's a harsh reality. But it's also a universal truth.

Chapter Ten
Overcoming Setbacks

How often in our lives are things going fantastic? Life is good in all areas: health, relationships, and finances. And then, boom. Out of nowhere, everything just seems to unravel on us. It is something that happens to all people; no matter what your stature in life may be, challenges and struggles can creep in, seemingly from nowhere. Life will always throw us our share of "bad bounces." The key to dealing with the bad bounces is what we do when they come our way. Here is a great example:

At Augusta National Golf Club on April 13, 2013, on the 15th hole of the 77th Masters Tournament, Tiger Woods was handed what many would say was the worst break of his career. A combination of a great shot that took a bad bounce and an error on his part would move him from the potential leader to starting the next day four off the lead.[31]

So Tiger finished the 2013 Masters tied for fourth place, four strokes off the leader, and a swing that cost him

---

31 Bob Harig, "2013 Masters—Tiger Woods Penalized 2 Shots," ESPN.com, updated April 13, 2013, http://espn.go.com/golf/masters13/story/_/id/9167230/2013-masters-tiger-penalized-2-strokes-ball-drop-15.

around $1.1 million in lost earnings for the weekend. What happened? How did he deal with such a bad bounce? Did he consider a major championship and a million dollars insignificant?

Tiger did exactly what he has always done in these situations. Earlier that year at Abu Dhabi, after missing the cut, something at that time that rarely happened to him, Tiger mounted an overwhelming win in his next start at Torrey Pines. When we think back to 2006, when Tiger failed to make the cut for the US Open, he went on to finish second in his next start, and then to win an unbelievable seven straight tournaments, including two majors.

The question is: What allows someone to come back after suffering a bad bounce in life? We all go through things, whether in relationships, business, health issues, and so on. What allows one person to pick up and move on to great heights of success while others falter by the wayside, unable to recover from a bad bounce?

Tiger and other great achievers have three unique qualities that are common in these types of individuals. I hope following these three steps can help you overcome those bad bounces of life.

1. They don't look back

Winners in all walks of life take the bad bounce, shake it off, and move on. High performers realize there is little value in dwelling on what might have been. They realize the future holds all of the opportunity.

2. They focus on the good and forget the bad

Life is about choices. How we think and feel about things is a choice that we all can control. Successful individuals realize they can create their own world by what they think. Those thoughts can turn into positive actions, thus creating the world (and future) they've focused their thoughts on.

3. They always want to take another shot

One thing is certain about people that win: they always want another shot, especially if they don't succeed with the first one. Again, winners have the ability to move on and try again when a bad bounce comes their way.

Thankfully, the bad bounces we take don't normally cost us $1.1 million. But, the car breaking down when the rent is due, an untimely illness, and many other things can cause financial, mental, and emotional stress.

In 2013, I had my share of life's challenges; it was one of those years when you wonder what else could possibly go wrong. I was tempted to write one of those Christmas letters . . . you know the letter where your friends or family tell you about Fred's promotion, Mary getting a full scholarship after being named prom queen, and Junior finding a cure for cancer while being chosen to be the first eight-year-old in space . . . My letter would be one that would make you cry and most likely want to send me a check.

Here is that twelve-month period (get a hanky and read on):

Two days after Thanksgiving, I was on my way to my office and slipped in my garage, tearing my quad tendon completely from the bone. I lay on the garage floor, wincing in pain. Unable to move, I threw shoes and other items from my briefcase at the door, hoping to get my wife's attention. Thankfully, my dog Bagger Vance heard the thuds and ran to my wife . . . "Mommy. Quick. Timmy fell in the well again." Saved at last. I had to have holes drilled in my kneecap and the tendon reattached.

Due to the injury, I was forced to wear a full leg brace from hip to toe for twelve weeks, giving me a throwback to my childhood of surgeries and body casts. A physiologist's dream, that's what I am.

One and a half months later, in the same year, my father passed away. Unable to travel, I could not be with him in his last days or attend a memorial service for him.

As executor of his estate, I was forced to deal long-distance with the challenges that come with losing a parent, dealing with an estate, and five siblings. Enough said?

Also in January, my son lost his job due to a corporate change in the position he was in. That hurt me personally because he's my son, but also because he was working for me at the time of the loss. It was a financial burden, also, to help him get back on his feet (and a potential source of argument about whether I should help him or not. Everyone has an idea about how to raise your kids).

In August, I had gastric bypass surgery to correct my uncontrollable weight gain; over the last few years, I began to resemble Jabba the Hutt with out-of-control blood pressure, high cholesterol, borderline diabetes, and sleep apnea (other than that I was doing pretty good).

Two weeks after the surgery, I started having some bleeding. Thinking it was just after-surgery issues, I ignored it for a week and ended up in intensive care, losing five pints of blood over that week. I spent four days in the hospital while my wife was out of town. I was scheduled to meet her in my hometown to bury my parents (I would have to miss this again).

Stay with me. There's more . . .

Three days after I left the hospital, my company notified me that due to corporate reorganization, my office was being eliminated and my services were no longer required. That was the first time in thirty-three years that I had ever been out of a job.

Due to that situation, we decided to sell our home (in a down market) and relocate.

Wow, what a year! Thankful? Blessed? What the hell do I have to be thankful for? Well, plenty. Everything happens for a reason and a purpose and serves us. This is something I personally choose to believe. Let me explain:

Tearing my quad, although painful and very inconvenient, actually helped me heal some very deep and old personal issues that had haunted me since childhood. I had been trying to resolve them; but going through the recovery process not only helped me with my knee, but helped me find closure . . . a blessing in disguise.

Having now lost both of my parents after the passing of my father, I'm an orphan at fifty-eight; and only someone who has lost both parents can understand that pain. Your parents are your parents, and you're still their child, even after they're gone. Some people may not think of it that way. So where is the good? For the past four years, my father had suffered with a broken heart from the loss of my mother, to whom he was married for fifty-five years. The pain of his loneliness was apparent whenever I was with him; and today, although I have lost him, he is at peace with my mother. That is a blessing I choose to accept.

In dealing with my parents' estate, I had the opportunity to honor my parents by helping to make their last wishes a reality. I hope they are proud of how I handled things.

The blood loss and ICU visit . . . Hey, I didn't die. It could have been much worse; I'm thankful it wasn't.

Regarding the loss of my job, my wife and I had tried to get back to the Carolinas for five years. Because of the events of the past several months, we have our dream home on a golf course in Greenville, South Carolina, and my son has been able to move to Florida, which was his dream.

Yes, I have much to be thankful for, as all of us do. Some say that as we go through life it seems like a random, chaotic mess of confusion with no rhyme or reason. But when we look back years later, our lives are like a finely written novel. I believe that is true. Remember, life is about choices. What you choose to believe is a choice. Look for your hidden blessings. They are there.

Chapter Eleven
Dress and Hygiene

It is said you only have five seconds to make a first impression. And that impression can set the stage for the relationship to follow.

This is not just my opinion. According to a consensus of the finest clothiers in the country, and the over 782 books on dress listed on Amazon.com, there are rules that must not be ignored . . . so don't kill the messenger.

When you want to dress professionally and make a great impression, it's the little things that count.

The Seven Deadly Sins of Business Dress and Hygiene:

1. Wearing shoes that are worn out and unpolished

You can be wearing a $2,000 Armani suit, but if your shoes are beat up, you may as well have gotten your suit at Goodwill. My wife has always told me, "Shoes make the man!"

2. Wearing suspenders and a belt at the same time

Braces (suspenders) and a belt serve the same purpose:

to hold up your pants. If for some reason you need to wear both, I would daresay you have a problem with your trousers. So pick one and only one! Oh, and clip-on braces are a big no-no . . . it's like a clip-on tie for God's sake.

3. Wearing a white dress shirt without an undershirt

You should always (and let me stress ALWAYS) wear an undershirt. I'm begging you . . . there are enough horrible things to look at in the world. Enough said!

4. Wearing a shirt that is not pressed

I don't care if you're in a hurry or don't have an iron. Take it to a dry cleaner. A pressed and crisp shirt is a must.

5. Wearing a tie that doesn't touch the top of your belt

If you have to hunch yourself over like Quasimodo to have your tie touch your belt, your tie is probably too short. It's not your fault? Your neck is too big? Hey, my neck (if you want to call it one) was twenty inches. It was more like a head sitting on a set of shoulders. Buy a tall man tie! All men's stores carry them. Just ask.

6. Wearing a short-sleeve shirt

Please, please, please, don't. If you are dressing for business and wearing a tie, that is. This rule could be negated if you live in Florida or are over ninety years old.

7. Wearing no overcoat in chilly weather

If the temperature is below forty-five degrees, you need an overcoat. There is nothing worse than seeing a well-dressed businessman standing on a corner shivering.

I hope I have not offended anyone, but sometimes the truth can be painful. The business world is tough enough. Give yourself every opportunity to win.

There. We covered dress, now let's talk hygiene. It's every bit as important as dress, maybe more so. Why should these things need to be discussed? You got me. But they surely do, and remember . . . don't kill the messenger.

1. Deodorize

I enjoy movies, and some unnamed actors might be famous for not wearing cologne or deodorant, but enough with the au naturel body treatment. If they want to sit around their own homes stewing in their own body odor, good for them; but if you're going out in public, deodorant and a little cologne would be appreciated. Nobody that I know gets turned on by another person's body odor, and unless I'm running with the wrong crowd . . . stink is still stink. Smelling and looking good is more of a mindset issue than anything else, but still . . .

2. Shower

A shower is mandatory at least once per day unless

you're in prison. If you are working with the public, how could you not shower daily? And, yes, I prefer a shower. But hey, that's me! As Kramer says on reruns of *Seinfeld*, "How could you sit in a tepid pool of your own filth?"

3. Trim those brows

Unless your goal is to have a family of birds or possibly rodents of some type set up shop in your eyebrows, a weekly trim is mandatory. My eyebrows get out of control weekly if I ignore them. So why would you possibly let them go unattended forever? Let me let you in on a little secret . . . they look ridiculous and everyone thinks so. Maybe no one ever told you, but consider yourself officially on notice.

4. Trim nose and ear hairs

When I started to realize years ago that I was losing my beautiful, naturally curly hair, I thought nature was making up for the loss by allowing it to grow like weeds out my ears and nose. Fortunately for me, my wife informed me that there was nothing even remotely attractive about having the world's longest nose hair. Please, if you want to make a good impression, don't give anyone cause to question what the hell is hanging out your ears or nose. Get a trim weekly. I'm sure your barber will be glad to help. Oh, and while you're there, do away with the unibrow, unless you're trying out for a *Star Trek* movie.

5. Manage your nails

So simple, but so often missed: Clean, trim, and file your nails, even if you work with your hands. You can take care of this one in that shower we talked about earlier.

6. Keep them pearly

White teeth, to me, are the ultimate sign of good appearance. You can have it all going for you, but if your teeth are the color of baked beans . . . well, I'm sorry it just doesn't cut it. I will confess, this one took me a while to get right myself. For most of my life, my teeth had a yellow tint to them. I would ask my dentist what I should do. He would reply, "Wear a brown tie!" Not funny. Finally I found a dentist who set me up with whitening trays, and my smile sparkles. Spend the money . . . it's worth it.

7. Take care of your breath

Realize there is probably a good chance your breath may smell bad. Even if you brush, floss, and gargle. It's not your fault . . . just do your best to be sure nobody faints because of your breath when you say, "Hi."

I joke about these issues, but believe me, they are critical to your success. Don't forget them!

Chapter Twelve
Adjusting to Change

I've never met a person, I don't care what his condition, in whom I could not see possibilities. I don't care how much a man may consider himself a failure, I believe in him, for he can change the thing that is wrong in his life any time he is prepared and ready to do it. Whenever he develops the desire, he can take away from his life the thing that is defeating it. The capacity for reformation and change lies within.

—*Preston Bradley*[32]

If fear is the single greatest thing that holds back most individuals in life, then change is the most difficult thing to implement in our lives. From changing jobs to things as simple as changing your hairstyle, change can cause emotional stress, depression, and great unhappiness in our lives.

The thing about self-improvement is, in almost every case, it requires change: whether changing our eating habits, financial spending habits, or destructive behaviors in our lives.

---

32 J. Kyle Howard, *The Tao of You*. (Arizen Phoenix Publishing, LLC, 2010), p. 128.

I have always believed that anyone can be successful, and that dreaming big, believing, and not giving up are key to success. I feel that life is about choices and success is a choice; it's still one of my strongest beliefs. But I was recently challenged regarding this belief. The person who challenged me is a mentor and someone I respect. We were having a conversation, and I made that statement to her about success being a choice. She questioned me by stating, "I know a lot of hardworking people who want to be successful but aren't, and they look for ways to change their lives."

The conversation soon turned to the meaning of success. Certainly, money cannot and should not be the benchmark of success; I believe success is truly subjective and takes varying forms. One very important thing that must take place in our lives for success to manifest itself is change. No matter what we are looking for in life, if we are doing everything mentioned in previous chapters (setting goals, having vision, passion, and persistence), if we are not willing to accept changes in our lives, our objective may be very elusive.

In my life, I have had to make many changes, and still have many changes yet to complete. I remember when I was turned down for my first insurance position. I had a chipped tooth, wild-looking hair, a sport jacket too big for me, and shoes that I can't even think about. Now, I had to stop and think about why I couldn't get a position in an industry that seemingly will hire anyone. Well, the bottom line was I had to make changes. Fortunately for me, I had a wife who must have seen some potential in me (thank goodness).

The thing I can tell you for sure is change is never easy, and most times, it will not happen overnight. The first thing that has to happen, once we accept that we need change in our lives, is to then determine what it will take to facilitate the needed changes.

My friend was right. There are so many people in this world that dream, work hard, and end up giving up. Sometimes it is very difficult to look in the mirror and be honest with ourselves. No matter what our situation or industry, questions that we must ask are:

1. **Do I have the proper skills?**
2. **Have I taken the time to learn about my industry?**
3. **Am I an expert in presenting what I have to offer?**
4. **Do I present myself well?**
5. **Do I have the right attitude?**
6. **Do I take the time to learn and improve myself?**

Certainly accepting change is the first step in making change; but the key is implementing the required changes. Part of implementing and accepting the needed changes is to understand two important things: First, what will you gain from making a change? And secondly, what will you give up to make the needed changes?

What you will gain is normally easy to understand.

Losing weight will allow you to have better health, a better self-image, and wear the clothes you have dreamed about. Changing an addiction will give you freedom to take control of your life. The benefits that change—positive change—brings with it are so plentiful that it is hard to understand why it is so difficult.

The benefits to change are not the problem. The problem lies in what must be given up. Whenever we change, we are forced to give something up and leave it behind. Unfortunately for most of us, we don't want to leave things behind, even when they are harmful to us. The familiar things we are used to, whether good or bad for our lives, are not easily abandoned. But abandoning those things to allow positive changes to come into our lives is worthwhile.

Chapter Thirteen
Finding the Right Vehicle

One great truth in the world is that many people work very hard their whole lives and find neither wealth nor happiness. One great misunderstanding is that through wealth one can find happiness. There is absolutely no truth to this thought process. You can see it every day when you look at the countless celebrities and wealthy individuals who, despite their wealth and fame, turn to drugs, alcohol, and sometimes even suicide. One of my favorite sayings is that money is only good if you plan on being alive tomorrow; and if you have to walk on this planet, it's better to have it than not. But to believe that wealth in and of itself will bring happiness will certainly leave you empty.

There is a famous old saying "success is the progressive realization of a worthwhile dream." Nowhere have I ever heard that money will equal success. I believe that to strive to have a better life or have more is not wrong. But it needs to be coupled with more than only money. How many lives we touch and how we live our lives are what matters. Our search for our great passion in life, the passion that lies deep inside and struggles to be released from within each of us, is what really makes a difference to us and to others.

Which is why your vehicle is so important (not the one you take to the store, but the one you use to reach your goals). In Chapter Eight, I explained "vehicle" as your career, whether you work for someone else, or you have your own business providing a product or service. This vehicle should also include your plan for advancement in your career (or knowledge of the structure of your industry that will help you get ahead), or in the case of your own business, your plan to start and grow that business.

I've met many people who feel unfulfilled in their lives as well as their work. To a lot of people, work is only a means to buy food to eat, keep a roof over their heads, and provide for other necessities.

That's why a lot of folks miss out on the great meaning and possibility deep inside their careers. And I'm not only talking about seeing the great purpose and impact that your work produces for others (although that is important). I'm saying that your career vehicle and passion are (or should be) closely tied together. One of the greatest "energizers" in life is to do work that gets you excited and out of bed in the morning. Because not only do you realize the impact your work has on others, you enjoy it and couldn't imagine a day without it.

But not a lot of people in this world have "work" like that. They feel that work is just work. They dream of getting out of their current career, but don't know what they want. Or they don't know what makes them passionate. Or they *do* know, and are afraid to act because of the possibility of rejection, failure, or some other outcome that could possibly be negative.

Sadly, one of the easiest things to do when faced with a problem is to do nothing at all. No wonder people are frustrated.

We don't have a guaranteed amount of time to live our lives. Some people prefer working for someone else and fulfilling their passions as a hobby on the weekends. Others prefer to have their passion (whatever drives and excites them) take a bigger role in their life, and it becomes their career.

Deciding to have a hobby or interest become your business seems easy. And although it can be enjoyable, the trick is making it profitable. Actually setting things up takes work. No one teaches a class in business school about what type of pickles to sell with your hamburgers, or what to do if the painting supplies arrive a week late for your life-size model airplanes, when you have an order for a client due that same afternoon. Learning these types of things is part of your vehicle, too.

Do you remember the line about passion from the song "Flashdance . . . What a Feeling" by Irene Cara, that I mentioned in Chapter Four? If it's so easy to discover your passion and set up a business, why are so many people frustrated, so often? Is it more than fear of the unknown, or rejection? I believe that there are three major reasons that individuals will not follow their dreams.

The first is fear, which we have discussed at length in earlier chapters. The second reason is that many people have never been told the importance of setting clear, defined goals. Yes, there are things they want out of life, but some folks just kind of hope they will happen. The third, and probably most important reason: I believe many people feel trapped in their lives. They are not afraid of failing; they just believe there is no chance things can change. Getting past this hurdle is vital because it stops so many peoples' dreams. It's like seeing no light at the end of the tunnel.

It is easy to accept life as it comes to us, but the price we pay in our soul when our lifelong dreams remain unfulfilled is equal to a living hell: a life filled with regret from what might have been. Do not allow your dream to die, no matter your age or your current circumstances. When your dreams are bigger than your fears, anything is possible.

Chapter Fourteen
Mentorship

Keep away from people who try to belittle your ambitions. Small people always do that, but the really great make you feel that you, too, can become great.

—*Mark Twain*[33]

When it comes to learning life's lessons, there is the easy way and the hard way. The easy way is getting advice and counsel from someone who has walked the path before you. There are so many individuals who are willing to advise and mentor others that it is a shame so many decide to take the hard way, which is learning as you go and learning by your own mistakes. Why would anyone choose that road? It's a mystery to me.

Learning from others is well and good, but where do we get advice, if and when we need it?

I have always felt that all I need for today is to be inspired; the rest of it I can figure out. The problem can be finding that inspiration. It is certainly true that motivation

---

33 Mark Twain, *Mark Twain at Your Fingertips*, ed. by Caroline Thomas Harnsberger, (Cloud, Inc., Beechhurst Press, Inc., New York, 1948), p. 354.

comes from inside ourselves; but inspiration helps spark the flame of that motivation.

When I first started in business with no experience, no ability, and certainly not the look of a professional financial services representative, I was a "ninety-day wonder." I set a record for sales for a new rep and ninety days later, everyone wondered where the hell I went.

You see, I left the business after setting a new agent sales record. Why? Because I allowed advice from individuals that did not have my best interest at heart to poison my mind. I questioned my ability to succeed. Bitter, complacent, veteran agents convinced me that my early success was just luck, that the insurance business was hard. Most people failed and so would I. Young, impressionable, and full of self-doubt, I fled back, on my own, to what I knew: the construction industry.

As I sit back now, after a successful thirty-three-year career with its ups and downs, I realize the great power that the words of one individual can have on another's life. Words can be positive or negative, and what is sad is when one person decides to use them to destroy another's dreams or aspirations.

Over my years, I have seen and met so many people who always want to give their advice. They have some great opportunity for you or want to tell you why what you are doing won't work. What I have learned over all of these years is to always look at "the fruit on the tree" of anyone that I am going to take advice from. What I mean by this is find out how they live their lives. Do they have good moral character? What type of lifestyles do they live? Are they happy? What do you feel is in their hearts?

Certainly, someone can be financially successful. But if he or she does not have moral character, is that what you want for your life? I have noticed that friends and relatives of young people want to protect them. So they give them advice and actually talk them out of following their dreams. Again, look at the fruit on the tree. This applies to all industries, or in any skill you may seek advice about, whether in business or your personal life.

In today's ever-changing, fast-paced world, we can oftentimes find ourselves questioning our strategy and direction. If we think back to our youth, many of us were fortunate to find that special person who, for some reason, took an interest in our success. It could have been a teacher, coach, or Scout leader. It was someone who had far more life experience than we did and was willing to share it and give guidance to us. In business, as adults, finding that same type of special person, who is willing to share his or her expertise, can save us much time and frustration as we build our careers and find our places in this world.

According to a survey by the American Society for Training and Development, "seventy-five percent of private sector executives said a mentor had been critical in helping them reach their current position."[34]

---

34 Dana Hagenbuch, "Finding a Guide: The Value of Having a Professional Mentor," https://www.experience.com/alumnus/article?article_id=article_1225291932545&channel_id=nonprofit&source_page=additional_articles.

You're never too old or too young to have a mentor. Here are five ways a mentor can help your career and life:

1. An experienced mentor who has walked in your proverbial shoes can save you invaluable time on the learning curve. Why learn the hard way if there are experienced individuals to guide you on the path?

2. The right mentor who is committed to your growth and success can ask the tough questions that can push you to higher levels of success.

3. A mentor can help evaluate your business strategy before you hit a wall. He or she can say, "What the heck are you doing?" before you go too far astray from your goals.

4. A mentor can be a solid shoulder and voice of reason when we have no one to go to and are frustrated.

5. The right mentor can open doors that you never thought possible, by helping you develop new and rewarding resources and business contacts.

No matter what your position, age, or experience level, you can always grow and become better. Finding the right person to guide you as a mentor can help you achieve that.

We've talked about why having a mentor is wise. But how do you select the right mentor? Figuring this out is important: picking the correct mentor will be critical to your future development and success.

Mentors come in all shapes and sizes and can have varied backgrounds, life experiences, and communication styles.

So where do you start? You start with yourself! The first steps in developing a mentor relationship are to understand the following things about yourself:

1. What do you want to accomplish in life? Do you want to be a successful sales representative, a teacher, a business leader, or something else? Determining what you want will be key to finding the right mentor.

2. What do you expect from a mentor relationship? It's important that you communicate your objectives clearly so that you are not disappointed.

3. What are you willing to do to achieve your goals in point number one, above? Are you willing to accept advice, even if it means change? If not, you may need to reconsider whether a mentor is the right step for you.

So you know what you want, and what you're willing to do to get there. How do you select a mentor?

1. Look at "the fruit on the tree." I mentioned this before when we talked about accepting advice from other people. When you select a mentor, it's just as important. Your mentor should have many of the qualities that you would want to emulate. Things like being successful, honest, having good communication skills, and having a good moral foundation.

These qualities are not always obvious, but if you look, ask questions, and do your homework, you can find out what kind of person you are considering.

2. Look for someone in your field or the field you are

aspiring to go into. Also, find someone local or nearby if possible so you can meet face-to-face as needed.

3. Listen to your gut. Most times you can get a feeling for someone. If your senses say stay away . . . listen.

A mentor relationship can be a wonderful and rewarding experience. It, however, is like everything else in life: you will get out of it what you put into it.

I certainly advocate having mentors, advisors, and life coaches. I have several individuals, even today, that I turn to for counsel. The key is to try to understand what their motivation is.

I learned a long time ago that if you help enough people to get what they want out of life, you will get what you want.

CHAPTER FIFTEEN

Persistence and Determination

If you've read this far, you might feel as if I'm a bit of a broken record. The same concepts have come up in several chapters. But that's my intention. There is no magic to becoming successful and having your dreams come true. The principles to being successful, in life as in business, are timeless and simple. So simple in fact, that most of us either miss them completely or just plain refuse to believe them.

As I mentioned earlier, my wife, Rose, and I have a box. We put pictures and notes inside it of things we want in life. Now, as crazy as it may sound, everything we have put in the box we have either gotten or are working toward getting. Call me crazy, but it works. Seeing and believing will make things happen in your life.

There are three great ideas that, woven together, form the fabric of success. I call them "The Three P's of Success." They are:

1. Planning

What do you want? What does it look like? What will it

feel like when you get it? What are you willing to do to get it? What is your plan or vehicle to help you get it? Folks, this is absolutely the first and most fundamental rule in getting what you want out of life.

2. Passion

We have to become passionate about what it is we want out of life. If we do not find a deep-rooted, burning desire to accomplish what it is we want, then anything or anybody can steal our dreams from us. Passion is the great spice of life.

3. Persistence

I don't believe that we ever fail at anything; we either do it or we don't do it. What I mean is, somewhere along the way we decide it is not worth the effort and we quit trying. As long as we never quit trying, we never fail.

One of my favorite statements about persistence is attributed to former President Calvin Coolidge:

> Nothing in the world can take the place of persistence. Talent will not; nothing is more common than unsuccessful men with talent. Genius will not; unrewarded genius is almost a proverb. Education will not; the world is full of educated derelicts. Persistence and determination alone are omnipotent.[35]

---

35 "Quoting Calvin Coolidge: 'Press On'," Staff & Guest Blog, PBS, May 24, 2011, http://www.pbs.org/wnet/tavissmiley/blogs/staff-guest-blog/quoting-calvin-coolidge-'press-on'/.

Chapter Sixteen

Passion

I have read many articles and books that have caused me to think about the relationship between inspiration and action. These writings called into question the idea that inspiration is the catalyst to action. As I stated earlier, I have always thought that if someone were sufficiently inspired, he or she would take action. My recent reading challenged this belief, offering the alternative viewpoint that action, in fact, is the spark of inspiration.

As I thought about this idea, I must say it caused me to question my belief about inspiration coming before action. In looking at things that have inspired my life, they were not inherent within me. Most of my life's passions were things introduced to me. And over time and with action (working in these areas), I found inspiration from them. Certainly, I do not want to take an emphatic stance on this issue, but it is a great concept for us all to ponder. While we are thinking about it, let's find something worthwhile and take action. We never know where it may lead us.

Speaking of being introduced to things I became

passionate about, I'd like to give you an example about action and inspiration that involves golf (you might have guessed that one). In a recent issue of *USA Today*, I read a great article by Nancy Armour about the legendary Tiger Woods. To quote her:

"Woods is thirty-eight going on fifty, his body more broken down than a jalopy, with a rebuilt knee, a patched together Achilles and a back that bears the signature of a surgeon. No way he matches the Golden Bear [golfer Jack Nicklaus] let alone passes him."

She goes on to state:

"For all that's ailed him, he has one body part still intact, and it's the most important one: his mind."[36]

Wow, what a concept! Here's the greatest golfer of all time (and, yes, I will fight you over that one) and his most important body part is his mind. What does that say about each one of us in our life's journey? Our minds are our most important tools in life, no matter where that life may take us.

Tiger realized all of this himself, as well. Just listen to how he closed his interview when he announced he would not play in the upcoming Masters due to recent back surgery:

"There are a couple [of] records by two outstanding individuals and players that I hope one day to break. As I've said many times, Sam [Snead] and Jack [Nicklaus]

36 Nancy Armour, "Skipping Masters will pay off for Tiger Woods," *USA Today*, April 1, 2014.

reached their milestones over an entire career. I plan to have a lot of years left in mine."

I, for one, wouldn't bet against the man. Whatever the mind can conceive, the body can achieve. Tiger Woods has the talent, work ethic, determination, and passion to own every record in the history of modern golf. The thing that I got from this article was here's a man that is dangerous in his sport because he believes in himself and sees what he wants. Are you dangerous in your life's endeavors? To me, "dangerous" means being passionate beyond what the obstacles are, and motivated beyond what you can see with your eyes.

There is no doubt that passion can make us "dangerously" successful in whatever endeavor we take on in life. Passion can drive us toward the persistence and determination we talked about in the previous chapter. Nancy Armour said that Woods had the one body part healthy that he really needed for golf: his mind. I'm not sure if passion comes from the mind or the heart. Most likely, I believe, the two are linked together. Passion is contagious and can be seen in someone's demeanor, words, and actions. Passion not only moves an individual, but those around that individual.

Here is the big takeaway: If you are passionate about something in your life, then take action immediately and let that passion propel you to unlimited heights of happiness and success. If you feel that you are passionate about nothing, find something that interests you and take action! Dive into it with everything you have and the passion will follow. Maybe action and inspiration are like the old chicken-and-egg scenario, or maybe not. You owe it to yourself and your future to find out.

CHAPTER SEVENTEEN

The Value of People

Why is it that so many people believe if it is legal then it is okay, regardless of the moral consequences that come with a decision?

I certainly realize what a sensitive discussion this can open up. The struggle between legality and morality crosses almost every facet of our lives, and the arguments on both sides are passionate and at times vicious. In this chapter, I want to focus on business and stay away from any social issues.

To me and my simple mind, it boils down to this: Is anyone getting hurt unjustly by what is being done? In my world, a fast-talking "slickster" can get anyone to sign anything, if the timing is right. The ramifications of signing can destroy an innocent person or family, but it can be perfectly legal.

The hardest issue to deal with in looking at morality is that it lies in the heart and soul of all men and women; it is not something you and I can control in someone else. Sadly, all moral or legal issues, at their core, stem from want: the desire for one to possess something that another has or may have. Revenge, money, love, or possessions, all of these are things that can lead one to either break the law or ignore social morality.

Crimes of greed are all too common today. We see them all the time on the national news. But what truly pains my soul is to see morally bankrupt individuals hide behind the law and, with a clear conscience, destroy others.

It is this simple: in any decision, ask this question "Is anyone getting hurt by what I am doing?" If you ask this and then follow your moral compass, you will find peace.

I find it hard to believe that anyone can truly value another human being and cross the line between legal and moral. Again, it is an issue that lies in the core of a person. And in the end that is truly what a person is.

Unless you live in a cave and are totally isolated from mankind, the value of other people in our lives can't be calculated. The interaction that we have with others on a daily basis has deep ramifications for the attitude of the entire world. A simple angry word or kind word has the power to influence someone's day. Whoever hears that word will in turn influence someone else's day, and so on.

I don't feel it is possible to discuss the value of people without looking at the word "hate." This word, unfortunately, is used too often to describe people in life that have affected us negatively. It is a word I dislike and try not to use, but unfortunately have used, I must admit. It is a word filled with evil, and if we truly value our fellow man, we should strike this word from our vocabulary.

What if I walked up to you, right now, and told you I hated you? How can I possibly hate you? I don't even know you. Well, first of all, you are correct. I don't know you. Secondly, if I told you I hated you, wouldn't it get your attention? That's what hate does.

But if I really did hate you, here are common reasons why:

1. **Because I think you're responsible for all my problems.**
2. **Because I think you want something that is mine.**
3. **Because I think you think you're better than me.**
4. **Because I think you hate me.**

The key words above are "I think." They say that our perception is our reality, and that is true; but the problem is that perception is not, in fact, truth. So often in business and life, we perceive one of the above, based on nothing factual. This can lead to many kinds of thoughts, from concern and worry, to anger and, yes, hate.

So much of the social hatred in today's world is based on the perception that one group of people has about another group; and so much of it is unfounded, on both sides.

Business can be the same way. Sales agents from one company have perceptions about sales agents from another company. And this can lead to ill-informed and unfair sales tactics.

I don't have the answer to this problem, whether on the social or business level. I believe hate is a terrible emotion that hardens and poisons the mind, the heart, and the soul. Carrying hate can add emotional and physical stress to our bodies and lives.

We control what we think and what we believe. When we understand this, our perceptions can be totally different. Once that's done, our emotions can change and hatred can be no more. Controlling our thoughts and beliefs is vital to truly appreciating the value of others and how they can be a positive influence in our lives.

I want to pose a question to you. Why is it seemingly so easy to be cruel and angry toward another person, when it is just as easy to be civil, and even kind?

We see it everywhere, every day, and in the most unlikely places. The person mistreating the other has never seen that person and knows nothing at all about that person's situation. In the coffee shop, someone yells at the server because the line is moving too slowly; a person gets in the wrong lane in traffic and someone behind that car goes into a rage. The smallest things seem to set off individuals today, causing public displays of childishness.

So, just what is it that makes individuals lose their cool so easily? This behavior doesn't help the situation and certainly cannot be healthy—physically or emotionally.

One thing that I have figured out is that it is impossible to be angry (or sad) and happy at the same time. If you are getting angry over something and you stop a moment and think of something cheerful in your life, it is impossible for you to stay angry; the two emotions just can't exist in our minds simultaneously.

Another thing that I have discovered is that anger is exhausting, draining me both physically as well as emotionally. On the other hand, kindness is energizing and rewarding. Every time I do even the smallest act of kindness for another person, I feel better—better about myself and the world around me.

So, I'm still confused . . . if you cannot be angry and happy at the same time, and it is so much better physically and emotionally to be happy and kind toward others, then why do so many still choose anger?

The question is not an easy one to answer and could be impossible to ever truly understand. It could have to do with one individual's need to feel control over another, and only through anger can they feel that control. Perhaps rage is an emotion that has been with them since childhood and is the form of expression most easily drawn upon. Whatever the cause, it is destructive to the individual being mistreated, the person who is showing the aggression, and everyone around them.

If we all can try to find something good to say or do for everyone we come into contact with, as hard as this is sometimes, the world will be better. We will be better.

But why do people want to control others in the first place? Tenzin Gyatso, the fourteenth Dalai Lama, was quoted as saying, "The foundation of Buddha's teachings lies in compassion, and the reason for practicing the teachings is to wipe out the persistence of ego, the number-one enemy of compassion."[37]

In my life's journey, the one key that I have discovered that has held me back in my dealings with others and stopped me from truly valuing what others bring into my life is my ego. I feel it is fitting to take some time to discuss ego and the negative power it can have on our growth in the world.

If you help enough other people get what they want out of life, you will get all you want and more. This statement rings true in all aspects of business and life, from selling products and managing and leading individuals, to taking over the carpool for soccer games and making dinner. If you take your eyes off yourself and always do what is right for those that you are dealing with, you will be successful.

So, why is this (sometimes) such a difficult concept for many to implement? One word: ego, the Latin word meaning "I." I have neither the education nor time to get into a philosophical dialogue on ego. You certainly could start a long discussion about Freud's concept of "id" and "superego" and how they interact. Again, I don't have the credentials to have that discussion; so, to simplify, let's just agree that we all have an ego, some small, and some . . . not so small.

---

37 "Dalai Lama Quotes," http://www.dalailamaquotes.org/the-foundation-of-the-buddhas-teachings-lies-in-compassion-and-the-reason-for-practicing-the-teachings-is-to-wipe-out-the-persistence-of-ego-the-number-one-enemy-of-compassion/.

Ego is a critical part of our success when it comes to prospecting in business. A big, strong ego can help overcome rejection and allow an individual to look at rejection as a challenge for themselves. Saying things like "I can set this appointment" and "I can overcome that objection" are vital to the career of any successful salesperson. More than that, it's part of a can-do attitude that will serve you at home and with friends, as well as at work, whether you have your own business or work for someone else.

However, ego can be destructive when we begin to believe that the "I" is all-knowing: that I have all the answers, I know the best way to do this, I don't need to learn anything, and my way is the only way.

Over my career, I have seen this kind of thing all too often. People who were otherwise very competent, experienced professionals, started allowing their success to overcome their empathy for their clients. They stopped doing ongoing discovery and allowed themselves to believe they had all the answers and didn't need to continue to research, learn, and grow. The client suffered in the end.

When ego takes over in our lives, the "I" becomes the most important thing in our world. Satisfying the "I" can destroy our business, our family, and ultimately our long-term success and happiness.

How can we keep our ego in check? Here are some things to keep in mind:

1. **You don't always have to be right.**
2. **You don't know everything.**

Don't ever feel you're the only one who knows how to do it best.

3. **Listen to those around you.**
4. **Always ask yourself "How will this affect the others involved?"**

A little ego can go a long way; too much can destroy us.

Never forget that people are an important and valuable part of our lives. How we interact with and treat others will eventually determine our success and long-term happiness. And never forget, true happiness and peace are found in *being,* not having.

CHAPTER EIGHTEEN

Taking Responsibility

> *A sign of wisdom and maturity is when you come to terms with the realization that your decisions cause your rewards and consequences. You are responsible for your life, and ultimate success depends on the choices you make.*
>
> —*Denis Waitley*[38]

Here is a quote from "Taking Responsibility," on the Vital Affirmations website. I couldn't say it better:

> This is a very important principle. As an adult, you are sole[l]y responsible for all the choices in your life. So many people look to blame others or circumstances for the things that are not right in their lives. This attitude is self-delusional; pretty much every long term situation that happens to us in adult life can be traced back to some decision or lack of decision made by us either at a conscious or subconscious level sometime in the past. Once we

38 Robert W. Mitchell, The Awakening Word: Being Called to the Spiritual Path. (AuthorHouse, 2011), p. 62.

> stop denying, blaming and whining and accept that we had our part to play in the circumstance, then we are in a better position to move forward and to learn from our mistakes.[39]

One of the easiest things to do in life is to blame someone else for the problems that we have in our own lives. What happens when we do this? We become a slave to the person we blame. I have found if I take responsibility for what happens, then I do not have to be bound with the chains that come with harboring a grudge or blaming someone else for my problems.

You may be wondering: What does this have to do with my business, or my life? I believe it has everything to do with both of those things, because life can get in the way of us doing business; it's almost impossible to not let one interfere with the other at some point. Carrying anger, blame, and resentment around only affects your attitude in a negative way. And at the end of the day, attitude is what ultimately matters.

In my career, I have met many individuals who complain about their company or their manager, blaming them for the failure they are experiencing. Let me tell you this . . . I have gotten myself into more bad deals than I care to mention. And in every situation, I could point to someone else for being the person who was responsible for

---

39 "Taking Responsibility," Vitalaffirmations.com, http://www.vitalaffirmations.com /taking-responsibility.htm#.VKIY1V4AM.

whatever might have gone wrong. But what I choose to do is realize that no one ever forced me into any deal I ever got involved with. I always did it of my own free will; and if the deal was bad and I stayed in it, shame on me.

By taking the jobs and deals I did, I really can't be mad at anyone but myself. And you can't really stay mad at yourself for very long. I don't have to go through life angry at someone and allow that anger to grow and affect my future.

Let's evaluate our company and our manager for a moment:

1. Does my company offer a competitive product to the market that we serve at a good value, with good service?
2. Is my company financially sound?
3. Is my compensation plan fair?

If the answer is yes to all of the above, then you really have all you need from your company. Get to work.

Now, to the manager:

1. Is my manager fair and ethical, and does he or she follow the company guidelines?
2. Does my manager provide me with structured

leadership, or does my manager give me the freedom to manage myself?

3. Does my manager respect me as a person and treat me with respect as a professional?

Again, if these things exist then you need to look inside yourself. Remember, no one is perfect, and no one has all the answers (don't expect them from your manager).

You see, and this one is the tricky one, most of us need some structure and leadership. When it is provided and we are asked hard questions like "Are you doing the activities needed to be successful?" we tend to want to say we have bad leadership rather than being honest with ourselves. Remember, in most cases success will not come without a price. That price is (usually) stepping out of our comfort zone. Our manager's job is, in part, to force us to do just that.

Please understand that I certainly realize that sometimes personalities just don't work, and that there are some bad managers and not-so-great companies. That being said, we need to discern whether personalities, the company, or the manager is the problem. Maybe we are being tested (which is how we grow). Whether the situation is your fault or not, take responsibility and do something about it. Don't continue to blame the manager or the company. If you take responsibility and do what you need to do, success will follow.

These are only my feelings on this subject and are certainly open for debate.

I love asking salespeople to think about what it is they really do. Good sales agents get paid large sums of money by people we really do not know (the company) to make a promise to pay a sum of money to someone we do not know (the client) by a third party they don't know (the company). Wow, now that's a deep one.

Maybe you're not in the sales profession like I am. The concepts in this chapter still apply. Whether you have your own business, work for someone else, or are in another life situation, you're still responsible for making the most of your life. You still need to have a solid life structure (your "company"), as well as support from those around you (or your "manager" could be you, if you have your own business). You may need to create your ideal business and life structure (including overall guidelines, code of conduct, professional image, and more) based on the information given in this chapter. Treat the "company" section above as a jumping-off point for your business model. Even if that means doing your own research to create your own product or provide a service (which is beyond the scope of this book).

Most importantly, if something needs to be changed, it's in your power to do so, and will result in a positive change in your business and life, change it!

CHAPTER NINETEEN

Understanding Why Things Happen

Every March, the anticipation of the first day of spring brings new hope for the new year. April rolls in and the saying "April showers bring May flowers" fosters joy in the heart. As the dogwoods and azaleas start to bloom, it is plain to see what new beginnings the universe will bring to the world.

That same hope and anticipation can also be manifested in our lives if we will allow it. Just as winter turns to spring and spring to summer, changes in our lives can bring fresh, new opportunities. The dark and dreary death of winter soon turns to the new birth of spring. The death of an old relationship or career can turn to the birth of the true love of your life or the greatest career opportunity of all time.

At the writing of this book, I am currently experiencing several new beginnings in my life. In nature, when the old dies off, slowly a new and wonderful world appears, if we will just open our eyes to it. One of my most exciting opportunities is the release of a new cover for my first book, *Showing Up to Play*. Realizing that the original cover was not telling the whole story of the book, my publisher and I made a business decision to allow the old cover to fade out and introduce a fresh look to my book. The new cover brings a renewed anticipation of success for the book and the lives I hope it will touch.

Sometimes things happen to us in life, and we don't understand, at least not right away. I believe that everything in life serves a good purpose for the future. It's important to carry forward in life with hope to achieve that future, no matter how difficult today might be. Keep your focus on the positive, as well as the possibilities, in your life, and you'll find success.